The ISO 9001:2015 Implementation Handbook

Also available from ASQ Quality Press:

The ISO 14001:2015 Implementation Handbook: Using the Process Approach to Build an Environmental Management System
Milton P. Dentch

ISO Lesson Guide 2015: Pocket Guide to ISO 9001:2015, Fourth Edition
J. P. Russell

How to Audit ISO 9001:2015: A Handbook for Auditors
Chad Kymal

The Art of Integrating Strategic Planning, Process Metrics, Risk Mitigation, and Auditing
J.B. Smith

How to Establish a Document Control System for Compliance with ISO 9001:2015, ISO 13485:2016, and FDA Requirements: A Comprehensive Guide to Designing a Process-Based Document Control System
Stephanie L. Skipper

ISO 9001:2015 Explained, Fourth Edition
Charles A. Cianfrani, John E. "Jack" West, and Joseph Tsiakals

ISO 9001:2015 Internal Audits Made Easy, Fourth Edition
Ann W. Phillips

ISO 9001:2015 for Small and Medium-Sized Businesses, Third Edition
Denise Robitaille

The Quality Toolbox, Second Edition
Nancy R. Tague

Root Cause Analysis: Simplified Tools and Techniques, Second Edition
Bjørn Andersen and Tom Fagerhaug

The Certified Six Sigma Green Belt Handbook, Second Edition
Roderick A. Munro, Govindarajan Ramu, and Daniel J. Zrymiak

The Certified Manager of Quality/Organizational Excellence Handbook, Fourth Edition
Russell T. Westcott, editor

The ASQ Auditing Handbook, Fourth Edition
J. P. Russell, editor

To request a complimentary catalog of ASQ Quality Press publications, call 800-248-1946, or visit our website at http://www.asq.org/quality-press.

The ISO 9001:2015 Implementation Handbook

Using the Process Approach to Build a Quality Management System

Milton P. Dentch

ASQ Quality Press
Milwaukee, Wisconsin

American Society for Quality, Quality Press, Milwaukee 53203
© 2017 by ASQ. Printed in 2016
All rights reserved.
Printed in the United States of America
21 20 19 18 17 16   5 4 3 2

Library of Congress Cataloging-in-Publication Data
Names: Dentch, Milton P., 1942– author.
Title: The ISO 9001:2015 implementation handbook : using the process approach
   to build a quality management system / Milton P. Dentch.
Description: Milwaukee, Wisconsin : ASQ Quality Press, [2016] | Includes
   bibliographical references and index.
Identifiers: LCCN 2016023938 | ISBN 9780873899383 (hardcover : alk. paper)
Subjects: LCSH: ISO 9001 Standard—Handbooks, manuals, etc. | New
   products—Quality control—Standards—Handbooks, manuals, etc. |
   Industrial management—Standards—Handbooks, manuals, etc.
Classification: LCC TS156.17.I86 D46 2016 | DDC 658.5/62--dc23
LC record available at https://lccn.loc.gov/2016023938

No part of this book may be reproduced in any form or by any means, electronic, mechanical, photocopying, recording, or otherwise, without the prior written permission of the publisher.

Publisher: Seiche Sanders
Acquisitions Editor: Matt Meinholz
Managing Editor: Paul Daniel O'Mara
Production Administrator: Randall Benson

ASQ Mission: The American Society for Quality advances individual, organizational, and community excellence worldwide through learning, quality improvement, and knowledge exchange.

Attention Bookstores, Wholesalers, Schools, and Corporations: ASQ Quality Press books, video, audio, and software are available at quantity discounts with bulk purchases for business, educational, or instructional use. For information, please contact ASQ Quality Press at 800-248-1946, or write to ASQ Quality Press, P.O. Box 3005, Milwaukee, WI 53201–3005.

To place orders or to request a free copy of the ASQ Quality Press Publications Catalog, visit our website at http://www.asq.org/quality-press.

∞ Printed on acid-free paper

Quality Press
600 N. Plankinton Ave.
Milwaukee, WI 53203-2914
E-mail: authors@asq.org
The Global Voice of Quality®

Table of Contents

List of Figures and Tables . . . . *vii*
CD Contents . . . . *ix*
Preface . . . . *xi*

Chapter 1 ISO 9000 History and Chronology 1

Chapter 2 The QMS as a Process 5
   Summary: ISO 9001:2015 Changes from ISO 9001:2008 6

Chapter 3 ISO 9001:2015 Requirements 13
   1 Scope 13
   2 Normative References 14
   3 Terms and Definitions 14
   Clauses 4–10 14

Chapter 4 Clause 4: Context of the Organization 15
   4.1 Understanding the Organization and Its Context 15
   4.2 Understanding the Needs and Expectations of Interested
       Parties 15
   4.3 Determining the Scope of the Quality Management System 17
   4.4 Quality Management System and Its Processes 18

Chapter 5 Clause 5: Leadership 25
   5.1 Leadership and Commitment 25
   5.2 Policy 27
   5.3 Organizational Roles, Responsibilities and Authorities 30

Chapter 6 Clause 6: Planning 33
   6.1 Actions to Address Risks and Opportunities 33
   6.2 Quality Objectives and Planning to Achieve Them 39
   6.3 Planning of Changes 40

Chapter 7 Clause 7: Support 43
   7.1 Resources 44
   7.2 Competence 47
   7.3 Awareness 48
   7.4 Communication 48
   7.5 Documented Information 49

Chapter 8 Clause 8: Operation 57
   8.1 Operational Planning and Control 59
   8.2 Requirements for Products and Services 59

8.3	Design and Development of Products and Services	63
8.4	Control of Externally Provided Processes, Products and Services	68
8.5	Production and Service Provision	72
8.6	Release of Products and Services	73
8.7	Control of Nonconforming Outputs	73
	Service Provisions and ISO 9001:2015	78

Chapter 9 Clause 9: Performance Evaluation **85**
- 9.1 Monitoring, Measurement, Analysis and Evaluation 87
- 9.2 Internal Audit 90
- 9.3 Management Review 95

Chapter 10 Clause 10: Improvement **99**
- 10.1 General 99
- 10.2 Nonconformity and Corrective Action 100
- 10.3 Continual Improvement 102

Chapter 11 Interpretation Guidance: ISO 9001:2015 Standard **105**
- Clause 6.1, Actions to Address Risks and Opportunities 105
- A1 Structure and Terminology 108

Appendix A ISO 9001:2015 Gap Analysis **113**
- ISO 9001 Chronology 113
- ISO 9001:2015 as a Process 113
- Transitional Periods of ISO 9001:2015 114
- Context of the Organization and Expectations of Interested Parties 114
- Integration of the QMS into the Business Processes 116
- Actions to Address Risks and Opportunities 116
- Top Management Commitment 118
- Organizational Knowledge 119
- Documentation 120
- Programs to Achieve Quality Objectives 120
- Preparing for Upgrade Audit to ISO 9001:2015 122

Appendix B Failure Modes and Effects Analysis (FMEA) **123**
- FMEA Example 126

Appendix C Stage-Gate® Idea-to-Launch Model **127**
- How Does a Stage-Gate® Process Work? 128
- The Stages 128
- The Gates 129
- Flexible Implementation into an Organization 130

Appendix D Quality in Healthcare: Five Whys and Five Hows **131**

Appendix E What Is Six Sigma? **133**

Appendix F What Is Lean? **135**

Appendix G Context of the Organization: Checklists for External and Internal Issues and Interested Parties **137**

References 139
Index 141
About the Author 147

List of Figures and Tables

Figure 2.1	Plan-do-check-act cycle	5
Figure 2.2	The quality management system as a process	6
Figure 4.1	Model of a process-based QMS	19
Figure 4.2	Generic manufacturing process	20
Figure 4.3	Injection molding process chart	21
Figure 4.4	Nonconforming process	22
Figure 7.1	Clause 7: Support	44
Table 7.1	Focus of clauses for competence, awareness, and communication	48
Table 7.2	Example of a records list	54
Figure 8.1	Clause 8: Operation	58
Figure 8.2	Understanding customer requirements and determining capability	60
Table 8.1	Examples of metrics for sales process	62
Figure 8.3	Design process	65
Figure 8.4	Design Stage-Gate process	66
Table 8.2	Contents of forms in design Stage-Gate process	67
Figure 8.5	Externally provided processes	69
Figure 8.6	Production and service processes	74
Table 8.3	Clause applicability for service	79
Figure 8.7	Flowchart: software developer	81
Table 8.4	Applicable ISO 9001:2015 clauses for software developers	82
Figure 9.1	Monitor and improve	86
Table 9.1	Internal audit plan for a process-based audit	91
Figure 9.2	Process diagram	92
Figure 9.3	Injection molding process diagram	93
Figure 9.4	Sample check sheet for clause 8.5, Production and service provision	94
Table 10.1	Examples of find-and-fix corrective actions	100
Table 11.1	Terminology differences between ISO 9001:2008 and ISO 9001:2015	109
Figure B.1	FMEA example	125
Figure C.1	The Stage-Gate product innovation process	127
Figure C.2	The stages	128
Figure C.3	The gates	129

CD Contents

Design Stage-Gate Process
ISO 9001:2015 Context Check Lists: External, Internal Issues and Interested Parties
ISO 9001:2015 Gap Analysis
ISO 9001:2015 Internal Audit Check Sheets
ISO 9001:2015 Risk Analysis Examples
Process-Based Internal Audit Plan

Preface

My first experience with ISO occurred around 1992. I was employed as the director of materials for worldwide film manufacturing at the Polaroid Corporation in Waltham, Massachusetts. The company was experiencing a big challenge: Polaroid's instant film products would no longer be sold in European hospitals unless the film was produced in an ISO 9001–certified plant. Since several million packs of instant film per year, plus many X-ray camera devices, were sold to hospitals in Europe, Polaroid needed to act quickly—and we did. Several engineers and managers were reassigned from their regular jobs to assist the film assembly plants in obtaining certification to ISO 9001. The film assembly plants achieved this goal in about a year, and instant film sales continued uninterrupted at the European hospitals.

Other than maintaining European film sales, what impact did the ISO certification have on the quality of Polaroid film? Judging from my observations, I would say very little to none. The folks assigned to implement the ISO certification were not part of the day-to-day operations in the plants; they attacked each of the 20 elements and attendant requirements of ISO 9001 as a short-term project with goals and milestones. Employees attended awareness sessions to be trained on how to answer questions from the ISO auditor: "What is Polaroid's quality policy? Where do you find instructions on how to make film? What steps do you take when film you made does not meet specifications?" The employees learned the answers in a somewhat rote fashion, and the auditors from Denmark were sufficiently impressed during their weeklong series of interviews and investigations to recommend the plant be certified to ISO 9001. While many nonconformances were brought up during the audit, the ISO team convinced the auditors that the film plant had addressed the issues with diligence and that Polaroid customers could be assured the film produced at these plants was of *consistent quality*.

In reality, Polaroid instant film, before and after ISO certification, was plagued with consistent quality problems stemming from its extremely complex scientific and manufacturing challenges. Customer experience with Polaroid instant film products over their entire 75-year life cycle indicated that one in four instant pictures was of poor quality. However, the perceived value of the instant experience was so great that customers purchased well over 100 million packs of Polaroid instant film every year until the late 1990s, when the advent of digital imaging essentially obsoleted it.

During the ISO audit in 1992, managers such as myself were instructed by the ISO team to stay out of the way—perhaps take some vacation time—as we had not attended the awareness (indoctrination) training. As materials director, I was responsible for coordinating the manufacturing planning and scheduling with Polaroid's sales and marketing divisions. In ISO terms, this process was referred to as "contract review" or sales-manufacturing forecast. Like many other publicly traded consumer product companies in the 1990s, Polaroid adjusted its film sales demand to satisfy Wall Street analysts for the quarter, with little connection to actual consumer sales demand. If the ISO auditor had asked me to explain the contract review process, Polaroid might never have been certified to ISO 9001! The ISO team selected lower-level employees to answer the auditor's questions, using professionally presented spreadsheets indicating a strong link between sales and manufacturing.

My opinion of the value of ISO 9001 certification was shaped by this first experience and continued as I observed suppliers to Polaroid becoming certified to ISO without any obvious uptick in quality or delivery performance. There was a joke circulating in the 1990s that went something like this: An ISO 9001–certified company manufactured life preservers to size specifications using precise instructions and tight tolerances. Unfortunately, the technical department had selected cement as the material of choice, so the life preservers were useless. The ISO 9001 revision in 2000 addressed the "cement life preserver" issue by placing more emphasis on results and customer requirements.

After leaving Polaroid in 1996 to provide materials consulting, I found a new entry into the ISO world by way of a graduate program I attended on total quality management. One of the monthly modules in the program at the National Graduate School of Quality Management was "Introduction to ISO Auditing." To complete the course I had to pass the Registrar Accreditation Board (RAB) exam for ISO 9001 quality auditors. I passed the exam, and after a year of trial audits, I became certified as an RAB lead auditor. Over the next 20 years I completed over 500 audits for large and small companies in the United States, Mexico, Canada, Europe, and Brazil. While conducting these audits and providing dozens of auditor training classes, I continued to observe the many flaws in the ISO process I had first observed at Polaroid—but I also saw how the discipline of the ISO approach could provide value when properly implemented and audited. Through my work with a very wide spectrum of manufacturing and service organizations, combined with my previous work experiences, I have accumulated a reservoir of best practices—what works, what to avoid—and an ability to explain the sometimes convoluted requirements and intentions of standards issued by the International Organization for Standardization (ISO).

I wrote the *ISO 9001:2015 Implementation Handbook* with the following goals in mind:

- Provide guidance to organizations (both manufacturing and service) seeking certification to ISO 9001:2015

- Assist currently certified ISO 9001 organizations in upgrading to ISO 9001:2015, while improving their present quality management system (QMS)

- Provide guidance for internal auditors

- Provide guidance on interpreting ISO 9001:2015 requirements

- Suggest improvements on the formatting of the ISO 9001 standard

For organizations obtaining ISO 9001 certification for the first time, I suggest you view ISO as a tool to support your business processes—the linchpin for consistency and standardization. The *Handbook* is structured to guide your organization through the process necessary to connect your practices to the requirements of ISO 9001:2015. For organizations that are already certified to ISO 9001, with a voluminous quality manual and dozens of seldom-used procedures, I suggest you consider the upgrade to ISO 9001:2015 as an opportunity to rebuild your QMS into a helpful asset in managing your business. The *Handbook* will guide you through the steps in creating a solid QMS in support of your business.

At the end of each section describing the requirements for the clauses of ISO 9001:2015, I've included audit questions related to the defined clauses. In addressing these questions, the reader can evaluate the organization's conformance to ISO 9001:2015 requirements.

Note: The contents of ISO 9001:2015 have been paraphrased in this book. Paraphrased text by its very nature can introduce differences in understanding and interpretation. This book should be used in conjunction with ASQ/ANSI/ISO 9001:2015 *Quality management systems—Requirements with guidance for use*. The interpretations and paraphrasing of ASQ/ANSI/ISO 9001:2015 in the *Handbook* are not authorized by ASQ, ANSI, or ISO.

1
ISO 9000 History and Chronology

The concept of an international standard for manufacturing was introduced in Europe in the 1980s, led by initiatives from the United Kingdom, namely the British Standard, BS 5750, which provided requirements for companies engaged in quality assurance, production, installation, inspection, and testing. The development of the European Union encouraged more trade among European countries, and the need for product standards became apparent. ISO 9000 essentially replaced BS 5750 in 1987 and became a worldwide, auditable standard for manufacturing and service. Initially, ISO 9000:1987 included three subsets:

- *ISO 9001:1987*. Quality assurance requirements for companies engaged in design, development, production, installation, and service

- *ISO 9002:1987*. Quality assurance requirements for companies engaged in production, installation, and service; basically the same requirements as ISO 9001 but without the design of new products

- *ISO 9003:1987*. Quality assurance in final inspection and test; covered only the final inspection of finished product without concern for how it was produced

The purpose of ISO 9002 was to allow companies that based their products (or services) on customer designs to certify to ISO without addressing the design function. Unfortunately, many companies that did provide design services to their customers decided to "finesse" the system by not submitting their design process for third-party assessment by the ISO registrar's auditors. This issue was resolved with the 2000 revision, which eliminated ISO 9002, requiring all companies to seek certification to ISO 9001—and explain to auditors why their processes did not include design services. The inspection standard, ISO 9003, was also obsoleted in 2000 and is currently included in ISO 9001. (Note: ISO/IEC 17025 provides requirements for the competence of testing and calibration laboratories; it is outside the scope of the *Handbook*.)

The International Organization for Standardization (ISO) has a goal to upgrade its management standard every seven years. During the 28-year period from 1987 to 2015, ISO 9001 progressed through four revisions: ISO 9001:1994, ISO 9001:2000, ISO 9001:2008, and ISO 9001:2015, the current version released in October 2015. Organizations currently registered to ISO 9001:2008 will need to upgrade to ISO 9001:2015 before October 2018. For clarification, ISO 9000:2015 covers the basic concepts and language; ISO 9001:2015 sets out the requirements of a QMS, the focus of the *Handbook*.

A brief review of the previous revisions of ISO 9001 traces the evolutionary—sometimes revolutionary—transformation of ISO 9001. For readers recently engaged in QMS, as well as those who remember the genesis of ISO in 1987, a review of the original 20 elements of ISO 9001 might raise the question of how far QMS has advanced—or maybe how a somewhat simple concept can be confounded. The original elements of ISO 9001 were:

4.1 Management Responsibility

4.2 Quality System

4.3 Contract Review

4.4 Design Control

4.5 Document and Data Control

4.6 Purchasing

4.7 Control of Customer-Supplied Product

4.8 Product Identification and Traceability

4.9 Process Control

4.10 Inspection and Testing

4.11 Control of Inspection, Measuring and Test Equipment

4.12 Inspection and Test Status

4.13 Control of Nonconforming Product

4.14 Corrective and Preventive Action

4.15 Handling, Storage, Preservation and Delivery

4.16 Control of Records

4.17 Internal Quality Audits

4.18 Training

4.19 Servicing

4.20 Statistical Techniques

These elements were maintained in the 1994 revision, which, in a somewhat evolutionary change, attempted to help third-party auditors by requiring more clarity in documentation from the certified company. Unfortunately, many companies responded by creating even more procedures and documentation—often with little value added to the company's quality performance. The essence of both ISO 1987 and ISO 1994 was "document what you do, do what you document," where procedures were seen to be more important than results or improved quality. The ISO 9001:2000 revision was a somewhat radical move in that the focus was on customer satisfaction, process management, and continual improvement. The ISO 9001:2008 revision had no new requirements—just a continued emphasis on process management and customer satisfaction.

The current revision, ISO 9001:2015, strives to make ISO 9001 a major driver in the business model of the organization. ISO 9001:2015 adds requirements for the organization to demonstrate the integration of the QMS requirements into its business processes and also to provide risk analysis in support of meeting the quality objectives. Additionally, it requires organizations to consider external issues and interested parties that are relevant to the QMS, other than traditional customers, suppliers, and employees. External issues that could impact the organization's business strategy, such as new technology, potential market forces, and competition, are open to auditing in the ISO 9001:2015 scheme. Later chapters will describe how various organizations may address these requirements.

The ISO 9000 concept now has a 29-year history. The original version with its 20 prescriptive elements provided industries around the world with a disciplined approach to manufacturing products. Over 1 million organizations worldwide are now certified to ISO 9001. I believe the discipline of ISO 9001 has been very helpful in improving the quality of most products since 1987. Certainly many other quality initiatives such as statistical process control have contributed as well, but ISO was a major component in establishing consistency. The ISO 9001:2000 revision generated quality improvements by encouraging certified organizations to focus on customers and process management rather than procedures and documentation. ISO 9001:2015 adds focus on risk management and encourages the integration of the QMS with the organization's business as well as the expansion of top management's direct participation.

2
The QMS as a Process

The internationally recognized standard for quality management, ISO 9001 is built on the plan-do-check-act (PDCA) approach (see Figure 2.1). This is the operating principle of all ISO management system standards, including ISO 14001, the standard for environmental management systems.

Put in the context of quality management, the PDCA approach works as follows:

Plan: Top management establishes the context, scope, boundaries, and quality policy of the QMS. Quality objectives are selected and programs established to achieve the objectives. The core processes of the QMS and their interactions are determined. Performance indicators for the core processes are established.

Do: Production and service processes are implemented with controls maintained to ensure customer requirements are met. Processes supporting the core processes are implemented.

Check: The QMS is monitored and audited to measure performance against the organization's objectives and customer requirements. The performance and results of the QMS are reported to top management.

Act: Actions are initiated to correct deficiencies and improve the quality performance as indicated by the monitoring and measurement of the QMS results. Resources and employee training are provided as appropriate to ensure improvement of the QMS.

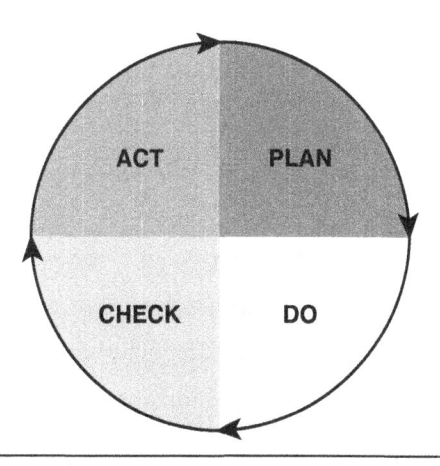

Figure 2.1 Plan-do-check-act cycle.

6 Chapter Two

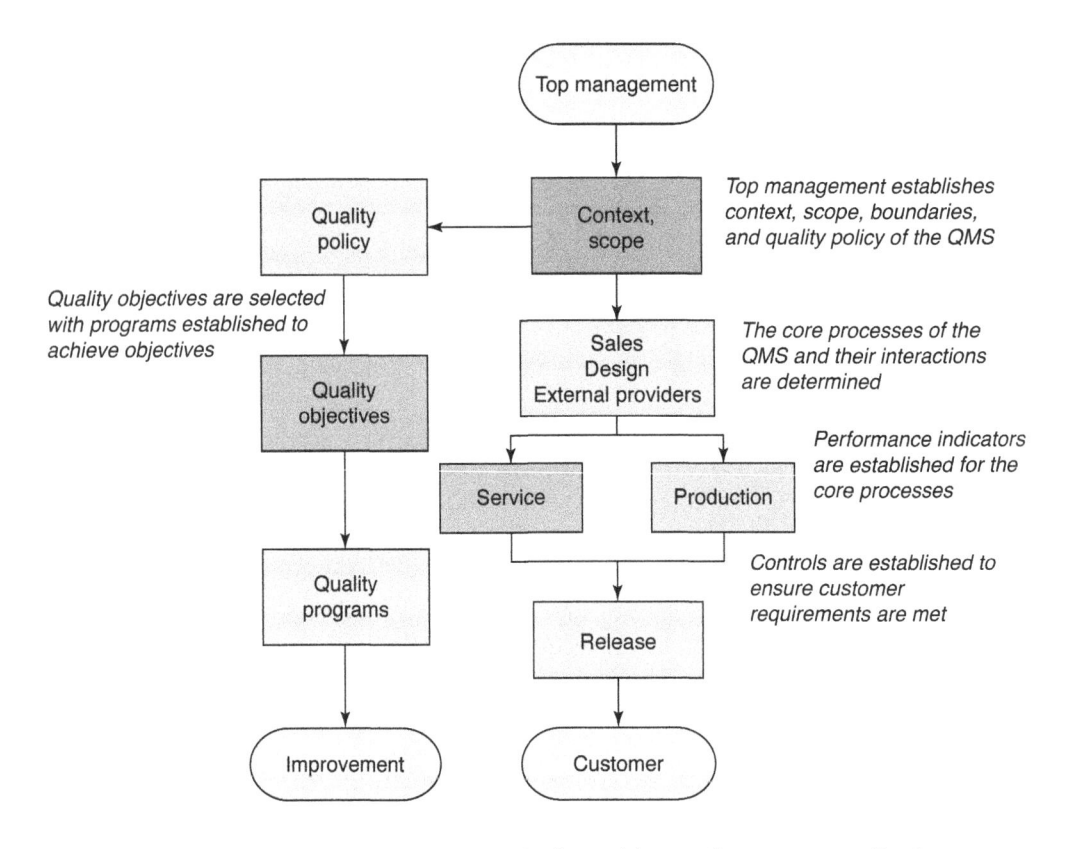

Figure 2.2 The quality management system as a process.

Support processes: Documentation, communication, training, quality assurance, calibration, maintenance, corrective action, internal audit, risk assessment, monitoring and measurement, management responsibilities, management review

While establishing the plans and actions to support a QMS, it is helpful to look at the QMS as a *process* with two desired outputs: improvement and customer satisfaction. The organization's management provides the inputs to the QMS process: scope of activities (business model) and the quality policy.

Figure 2.2 represents the core process of a QMS and is the starting point for building the QMS. The next step is to define the business model for the organization with linkage to related ISO 9001:2015 requirements. Chapters 4–10 provide guidance on establishing each process conforming to the related ISO 9001:2015 requirements.

SUMMARY: ISO 9001:2015 CHANGES FROM ISO 9001:2008

Organizations currently certified to ISO 9001:2008 will need to address the new (or expanded) requirements of ISO 9001:2015, including:

- Understanding the context of the organization and expectations of interested parties

- The integration of the QMS requirements into the organization's business processes

- Actions to address risks and opportunities
- Expanded top management commitment
- Organizational knowledge

Context and Interested Parties

Past revisions of ISO 9001 required organizations to define the scope of the QMS—the activities, processes, and buildings and property within their QMS. ISO 9001:2015 requires the organization to identify and monitor the internal and external issues as well as the interested parties that are relevant to the organization's purpose and its strategic direction. Organizations are now required to consider external issues that could impact their business strategy, such as new technology and potential market forces (e.g., social and economic environments, international competition). In a similar fashion, the organization should identify the interested parties that may be relevant to the QMS. Examples include the regulatory bodies administering statutory and regulatory requirements related to the product.

Each organization needs to address these requirements in the context of its business model. A company producing consumer products may have several areas of opportunity in its business strategy to address relevant external issues and the concerns of interested parties. In today's intensely competitive, global market, most consumer product companies already have initiatives in place to address product-related regulatory threats as well as global manufacturing competition. ISO 9001–certified organizations competing as discrete manufacturers (e.g., machine shops, metal or plastics formers, electronic and machinery builders) have fewer options. Considerations for these types of organizations include reviewing environmentally compatible material options, the latest technical innovations, and alternative manufacturing techniques.

Integration of QMS Requirements into Business Processes

Many ISO 9001–certified companies have integrated the QMS into their business planning and strategy. Companies of all sizes have woven the quality performance metrics into their business plan. Key performance indicators (KPIs) are assigned to quality and business parameters along with safety and environmental metrics. Quality-driven waste reduction projects include improved environmental performance. Best-in-class organizations have established a business management system (BMS) combining their financial, quality, safety, and environmental systems into a cohesive operational model. Some ISO 9001–certified companies, however, operate with their QMS at arm's length from their business—just doing the minimum required to maintain certification. The ISO 9001:2015 requirements should nudge these companies into broadening their perspective on creating an integrated business management system.

Actions to Address Risks and Opportunities

The requirement to provide risk analysis in QMS activities is a key difference in ISO 9001:2015 compared to previous revisions. The organization is now required to assess the risks and opportunities related to its purpose, its business strategy, and the expectations of interested parties to ensure the QMS meets its objectives. Quality tools currently used in many organizations include strategic planning process, strengths-weaknesses-opportunities-threats (SWOT) analysis, Six Sigma, and lean manufacturing programs. Results of the analysis should be used in establishing objectives and planning to mitigate the risks. Failure modes and effects analysis (FMEA) could be used. While organizations with an effective QMS certainly understand the risks related to their operations, the new requirements of ISO 9001:2015 may have a positive effect on many organizations by requiring a more formalized risk evaluation process and subjecting it to a third-party audit. It should be noted that ISO 9001:2015 does not have a requirement for preventive action. The reasoning is that the entire QMS is preventive in nature, as is the risk analysis approach. See Chapter 11 for guidance on documentation of risk analysis. Chapter 6 includes suggestions on how an organization might address the requirements for risk-based thinking.

Top Management Commitment

While the previous revisions to ISO 9001 included commitment from management to support the QMS, ISO 9001:2015 amplifies this requirement. The ISO 9001:2015 standard does not use the title "management representative" as previous ISO 9001 standards did. However, the organization can continue to use this title to convey certain responsibilities. The intent of ISO 9001:2015 is to emphasize top management's responsibilities as going beyond delegating. In my past experiences with a small group of organizations, management had delegated the quality management coordination too far down the organizational chart. This was evident when the quality management representative did not attend management review meetings to present the status of the QMS—not a good sign. Management's explanation for this was that financial and other sensitive issues needed to be discussed at the meeting, and the quality coordinator should not be privy to such information. ISO 9001:2015 requirements strive to prevent the overdelegation of QMS support and coordination.

Organizational Knowledge

ISO 9001:2015 Annex A, *Clarification of new structure, terminology and concepts*, addresses:

> The need to determine and manage the knowledge maintained by the organization, to ensure that it can achieve conformity of products and services. Requirements regarding organizational knowledge were introduced for the purpose of: safeguarding the organization from loss of knowledge, e.g. through staff turnover; failure to capture and share information; encouraging the organization to acquire knowledge, e.g. learning from experience; mentoring; benchmarking.

While ISO 9001:2008 clause 6.2, Human resources, subclause 6.2.1, General—"Personnel performing work affecting conformity to product requirements shall be competent on the basis of appropriate education, training, skills and experience"—implied that organizations should maintain organizational knowledge, ISO 9001:2015 requires organizations to consider and review the organization's processes to ensure that operational/process or product knowledge is maintained when employees leave the organization, and to review processes used by the organization to remain knowledgeable about new technology relevant to their business model.

A third-party auditor would expect the organization, depending on its operations, to have some formalized program for succession planning, technology updates, and supplier contingencies. Many ISO 9001–certified organizations have processes in place for maintaining organizational knowledge by way of their business strategy and contingency plan. The organization's internal auditors and third-party auditors will need to be sensitive to possible confidentiality issues with regard to this information. Additionally, since the clause requires the organization to "consider its current knowledge and determine how to acquire or access any necessary additional knowledge," auditors "should not require the organization to implement actions to acquire additional knowledge," as the implementation of a business strategy is confidential and outside the scope of ISO 9001 and the skill set of the majority of ISO auditors.

Other Changes

ISO 9001:2015 also has terminology revisions and expansion on previous requirements that should be considered:

- Documentation, terminology changes
- Programs to implement quality objectives

Documentation

A terminology change (not a new requirement) in ISO 9001:2015 is the modification of the clause numbering and documentation formatting. This change was made to achieve alignment with the formatting of ISO 14001:2015, *Environmental management systems*. (To help those who are familiar with ISO 9001:2008 make the transition, a table is provided at the beginning of Chapters 4–10 in the *Handbook*, matching the ISO 9001:2015 clauses discussed in that chapter to the corresponding clauses in ISO 9001:2008.)

ISO 9001:2015 Annex A states: "There is no requirement in this International Standard for its structure and terminology to be applied to the documented information of an organization's QMS." Organizations currently using documents, procedures, and quality records in their QMS should not feel compelled to adjust to the new terminology. Likewise, while the new standard does not explicitly require a quality manual, organizations currently maintaining a quality manual may want to continue using it as a high-level consolidation of the key elements—or road map—of their quality documentation (as was required by ISO 9001:2008). Organizations whose quality manual paraphrases each ISO 9001 clause requirement—going back through several ISO 9001 revisions—should seriously consider updating their quality manual to include:

- A description of the organization's business model, including the context of the organization and the expectations of interested parties
- The scope (the activities, processes, and buildings and locations) of the QMS

- A description of those ISO 9001:2015 requirements that are not applicable to the QMS, as they do not affect the organization's ability or responsibility to ensure the conformity of its products and services

- The documented procedures (documented information) established for the QMS, or reference to them

- A description of the processes in the QMS and how they interact

- The quality policy

- Responsibilities/authorities

Organizations looking to upgrade to ISO 9001:2015 should review Annex A to obtain a better understanding of the new terminology. Unfortunately, some guidance in the Annex is unclear. Chapter 11 discusses interpretation concerns.

Programs to Implement Quality Objectives

ISO 9001:2008 clause 5.4.1, Quality objectives, reads: "Top management shall ensure that quality objectives, including those needed to meet requirements for product, are established at relevant functions and levels within the organization. The quality objectives shall be measurable and consistent with the quality policy." The planning required to implement the quality objectives was somewhat vague.

ISO 9001:2015 clause 6.2.2, Quality objectives and planning to achieve them, reads: "When planning how to achieve its quality objectives, the organization shall determine: what will be done; what resources will be required; who will be responsible; when it will be completed; how the results will be evaluated."

While past revisions of ISO 9001 gave organizations some flexibility in implementing their quality objectives, third-party auditors will now expect the organization to have a defined program to achieve each of its quality objectives. This requirement is consistent with ISO 14001:2015 and should reduce auditing inconsistencies—and enhance quality improvements.

Auditing Notes

The evaluation of some of the new ISO 9001:2015 requirements will be somewhat subjective for third-party auditors. When will an organization be judged as nonconforming in addressing the requirements for context/interested parties, risk analysis, and top management commitment? If there are no examples of proactive initiatives related to addressing the needs of interested parties or external issues, will that be deemed a nonconformance? In my experiences auditing to the ISO 9001 standard, if the organization had not met its improvement goal the auditor did not issue a nonconformance as long as the organization either documented the reason the goal was missed or established actions to correct the situation. I would expect third-party auditors to follow this guideline when assessing performance against the new ISO 9001:2015 requirements. In the case of the requirement to determine the needs of interested parties and external issues, the organization should be able to provide documentation indicating that a review process is in place relative to the context of the organization and its business model. At a minimum, an organization would be expected to have some form of risk analysis process related to the QMS. With regard to assessing top management commitment to the QMS, an experienced third-party auditor will be able to detect when resources are not adequate to support the QMS and will issue nonconformances as applicable.

Transitional Periods of ISO 9001:2015

The ISO 9001:2015 standard was published on October 25, 2015. Companies that are certified to ISO 9001:2008 have three years to bring their QMS up to date with ISO 9001:2015. Eventually all certificates in accordance with ISO 9001:2008 will become invalid and will be withdrawn as of October 25, 2018.

Usually it is most efficient for both the organization and the ISO registrar to conduct the upgrade audit to ISO 9001:2015 during the organization's three-year recertification audit; however, the upgrade can be done during the annual surveillance audit.

Appendix A, "ISO 9001:2015 Gap Analysis," summarizes the changes from ISO 9001:2008. The gap analysis can be used to make staff aware of the new requirements of ISO 9001:2015.

3
ISO 9001:2015 Requirements

In its 2015 revisions, ISO applied the same structure to both *Quality management systems* (ISO 9001:2015) and *Environmental management systems* (ISO 14001:2015):

1 Scope

2 Normative references

3 Terms and definitions

4 Context of the organization

5 Leadership

6 Planning

7 Support

8 Operation

9 Performance evaluation

10 Improvement

ASQ/ANSI/ISO 9001:2015 *Quality management systems—Requirements* (as the US adoption is called) includes the Scope, Normative References, and Terms and Definitions sections as follows.

1 SCOPE

This International Standard specifies requirements for a quality management system when an organization:

a) Needs to demonstrate its ability to consistently provide products and services that meet customer and applicable statutory and regulatory requirements, and

b) Aims to enhance customer satisfaction through the effective application of the system, including processes for improvement of the system and the assurance of conformity to customer and applicable statutory and regulatory requirements

All the requirements of this International Standard are generic and are intended to be applicable to any organization, regardless of its type or size, or the products and services it provides.

Note 1: In this International Standard, the terms "product" and "service" only apply to products and services intended for, or required by, a customer.

Note 2: Statutory and regulatory requirements can be expressed as legal requirements.

2 NORMATIVE REFERENCES

The following documents, in whole or in part, are normatively referenced in this document and are indispensable for its application. For dated references, only the edition cited applies. For undated references, the latest edition of the referenced document (including any amendments) applies.

ISO 9000:2015, *Quality management systems—Fundamentals and vocabulary*

3 TERMS AND DEFINITIONS

For the purposes of this document, the terms and definitions given in ISO 9000:2015 apply.

CLAUSES 4–10

Sections (clauses) 4–10 provide the requirements for certification to ISO 9001:2015.

Note: In Chapters 4–10, the general requirements of each ISO 9001:2015 clause are paraphrased in the shaded boxes. **Boldface text** indicates a change from ISO 9001:2008. For organizations currently certified to ISO 9001:2008, each of these chapters begins with a table that matches the ISO 9001:2015 clauses discussed in that chapter to the corresponding clauses in ISO 9001:2008.

4

Clause 4: Context of the Organization

#	ISO 9001:2015	#	ISO 9001:2008
4	Context of the organization	—	NEW
4.1	Understanding the organization and its context	—	NEW
4.2	Understanding the needs and expectations of interested parties	—	NEW
4.3	Determining the scope of the quality management system	4.2.2	Quality manual
4.4	Quality management system and its processes	4.1 8.2.3	Quality management system General requirements Monitoring of processes

4.1 UNDERSTANDING THE ORGANIZATION AND ITS CONTEXT

> The organization shall determine external and internal issues relevant to its purpose and its strategic direction. The organization shall monitor and review information about the external and internal issues that affect its ability to achieve the intended results of its quality management system.

4.2 UNDERSTANDING THE NEEDS AND EXPECTATIONS OF INTERESTED PARTIES

> The organization shall determine the interested parties that are relevant to its quality management system. The organization shall monitor and review information about the interested parties and their potential effect on the organization's ability to consistently provide products and services that meet customer and applicable statutory and regulatory requirements.

These two clauses of ISO 9001:2015 have very different requirements than previous versions of ISO 9001, which required the organization to determine the scope of the QMS. **ISO 9001:2015** requires the organization to determine the scope of the organization's business. This is an attempt by the writers of ISO 9001:2015 to extend the ISO approach beyond the quality management of the organization into the business as a whole. In the past, ISO 9001 required a definition of the scope: the activities, products, and services of the organization. The subsequent clauses of ISO 9001 then introduced requirements to manage the QMS.

In addition to determining scope, organizations are now required to consider external issues that could impact their business strategy, such as new technology and potential market forces (e.g., social and economic environments, international competition). In a similar fashion, the organization should identify the interested parties that may be relevant to the QMS. Examples include the regulatory bodies administering statutory and regulatory requirements related to the product. Each organization needs to address these requirements in the context of its business model. A company producing consumer products may have several areas of opportunity in its business strategy to address relevant external issues and the concerns of interested parties. In today's intensely competitive, global market, most consumer product companies already have initiatives in place to address product-related regulatory threats as well as global manufacturing competition. ISO 9001–certified organizations competing as discrete manufacturers (e.g., machine shops, metal or plastics formers, electronic and machinery builders) have fewer options. Considerations for these types of organizations include reviewing environmentally compatible material options, the latest technical innovations, and alternative manufacturing techniques.

Appendix G provides checklists the organization can use to assess who the interested parties are and what external and internal issues could impact the organization.

Audit Questions

Clauses 4.1 and 4.2

What are the internal and external issues that are relevant to the organization's purpose and its strategic direction?

Examples: Legal, technological, competitive, market, cultural, social, and economic environments, whether international, national, regional, or local

How does the organization review and monitor the relevant internal and external issues?

Example: Business planning strategy

Who/what are the interested parties that are relevant to the QMS?

Examples: Legal agencies and regulatory bodies, creators of new technology, new competitors

How does the organization review and monitor the requirements of relevant interested parties?

Example: Business planning strategy

> **Audit Tip**
>
> One challenge for organizations and third-party auditors is how to maintain confidentiality when an organization's business strategy is being reviewed. If confidentiality is an issue, I suggest the organization present to the auditor the process used to establish the business plan, minus the implementation details. While auditors and registrars do sign confidentiality agreements with client companies, I believe an organization's business plans are too sensitive to share with people outside the company.

4.3 DETERMINING THE SCOPE OF THE QUALITY MANAGEMENT SYSTEM

> The organization shall determine the boundaries and applicability of the quality management system to establish its scope. The organization shall consider the products and services of the organization, the external and internal issues and the requirements of relevant interested parties when determining the scope.
>
> The organization shall apply and document all the applicable requirements of this International Standard within the scope of its quality management system.
>
> The scope shall state the types of products and services covered in the scope. Any requirement of this International Standard that the organization determines is not applicable to the scope of its quality management system shall be stated with justification for exclusion. Conformity to this International Standard may only be claimed if the requirements determined as not being applicable do not affect the organization's ability or responsibility to ensure the conformity of its products and services and the enhancement of customer satisfaction.

Clause 4.3, Determining the scope of the quality management system, is essentially the same as the 2008 requirements, with the addition of considerations of internal and external issues and interested parties. Also, in ISO 9001:2008, the organization was required to define and justify any exclusion (clauses). With ISO 9001:2015 the organization needs to apply all the requirements that are applicable within the determined scope. In reality, the scope requirements have not substantially changed.

> **Audit Questions**
>
> **Clause 4.3**
>
> *What is the scope of the QMS?*
> Scope is defined as the activities, products, and services of the organization.
>
> *What are the boundaries applicable to the organization's scope?*
> - Multiple buildings (addresses)
> - Multiple sites (locations)

18 Chapter Four

> *What manufacturing processes or services located at the site are not applicable to the organization's scope?*
>
> Examples: Design or service? Explain why these processes do not impact the organization's ability to meet the expectations of its customers.
>
> *How were external and internal issues and the expectations of interested parties, relevant to the organization's requirements, considered when the organization's scope was established?*
>
> Examples: Multisite manufacturing, international sales offices, design centers

4.4 QUALITY MANAGEMENT SYSTEM AND ITS PROCESSES

> 4.4.1: The organization shall establish, implement, maintain and continually improve a quality management system, including the processes needed and their interactions, in accordance with the requirements of this International Standard.
>   The organization shall determine the inputs and outputs expected from the processes needed for the quality management system and their application throughout the organization.
>   The organization shall:
>
> - Determine the sequence and interaction of these processes;
> - Determine and apply the criteria and methods to monitor or measure the related performance indicators needed to ensure the effective operation and control of these processes;
> - Determine the resources needed for these processes and ensure their availability;
> - Assign the responsibilities and authorities for these processes;
> - **Address the risks and opportunities in controlling these processes;**
> - Evaluate the processes and implement any changes needed to ensure that the processes achieve their intended results.
>
> 4.4.2: The organization shall maintain **documented information**[1] to support the operation of its processes and have confidence the processes are being carried out as planned.

Clause 4.4, Quality management system and its processes, has the same requirements as ISO 9001:2008 clause 4.1, Quality management system; however, there is a new requirement in **ISO 9001:2015** for the organization to *address risks and opportunities* within the QMS. Risk analysis will be discussed in Chapter 6.

Determining the *sequence and interaction* of the organization's processes has been one of the more confusing and misapplied aspects of QMS since the addition of this requirement in ISO 9001:2000. As a third-party quality auditor for the last

---

1. A nomenclature change with ISO 9001:2015 is designating "documented information" to cover both documents and records, which were defined independently in prior ISO 9001 revisions. This is consistent with ISO 14001:2015 and is intended to allow for a variety of media in documenting the organization's plans. Chapter 7 will review this terminology change further.

20 years, I have seen just about every process flowchart imaginable—some that were really great (and useful), but many more that were completely useless. For organizations currently certified to ISO 9001:2008, I suggest you consider whether the process flow and interactions chart that you have been using (with approval from your registrar's auditors) provides any value to your QMS. There are two parts to determining the sequence and interactions of the processes within the business model: the description of the processes and managing how they relate to each other. While a flowchart may describe what the processes are and arrows may indicate how they connect, it is not clear how the chart helps an organization manage its quality system or business, particularly if a machine shop has the same flowchart as a complex semiconductor manufacturer. I have seen the flowcharts shown in Figures 4.1 and 4.2 at various ISO 9001–certified companies.

The model of a process-based QMS shown in Figure 4.1 is from the ISO 9001:2000 standard and represents the interactions of the clauses of ISO 9001. When copied and pasted into an organization's quality manual, it does not represent the sequence and interactions of the processes within the organization's business. Likewise, the generic manufacturing chart shown in Figure 4.2 is often used and could be the chart for any manufacturing process—but it provides little value.

A properly designed process flowchart can be useful in training employees and establishing an outline for monitoring and controlling the processes. The

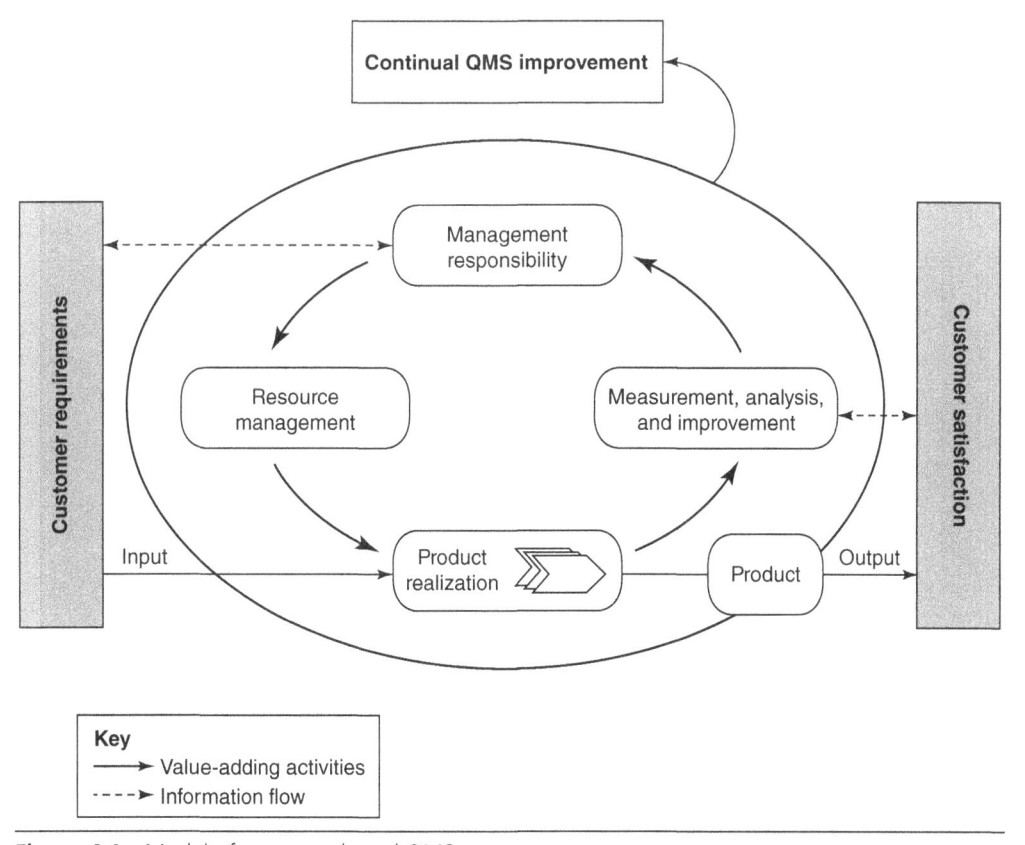

Figure 4.1 Model of a process-based QMS.

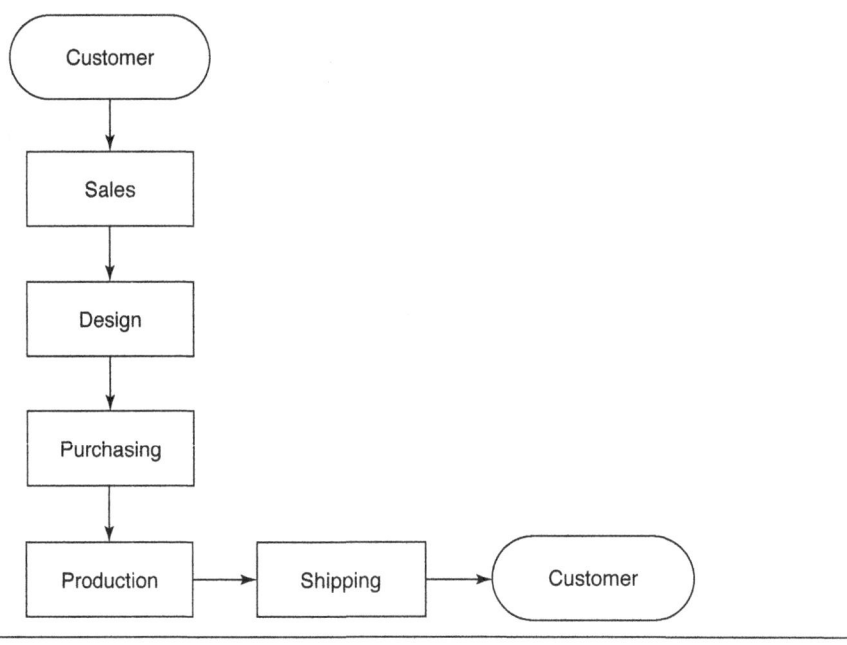

Figure 4.2 Generic manufacturing process.

flowchart shown in Figure 4.3 describes the processes in a company that produces injection-molded products. The processes are considered customer (or core) oriented, as each one has a connection to customer requirements. The QMS will also include support oriented processes: documentation, employee training, communication, corrective action, nonconforming products, internal audit, management review, and improvement. In addition, there are support processes related to maintaining the plant facilities and equipment, such as calibration and maintenance.

Contrary to popular belief, none of the of ISO 9001 revisions has required organizations to prepare a flowchart. Clause 4.1 of ISO 9001:2008 required the organization to "determine the processes needed for the quality management system and their application throughout the organization and determine the sequence and interaction of these processes." To satisfy this requirement, an organization could provide a list of its customer-related processes and describe how they relate to each other. For example, say the Jones Plastics Company produces injection-molded plastic parts. Their documentation identifies the sequence and interaction of the processes as follows:

> The Jones Plastics Company purchases resins and other materials. We ensure the materials meet our specifications. Our customers provide us with purchase orders defining the product part numbers, quantity and date needed, and other pertinent information. We use molding machines to melt the resins in molds provided by our customers with operating parameters established to match the customer-provided design requirements. Our machine shop prepares mounting plates for the plastic parts that are assembled to the plastic pieces. We inspect the molded products to ensure they conform to customer specifications and package and ship the products to the customers.

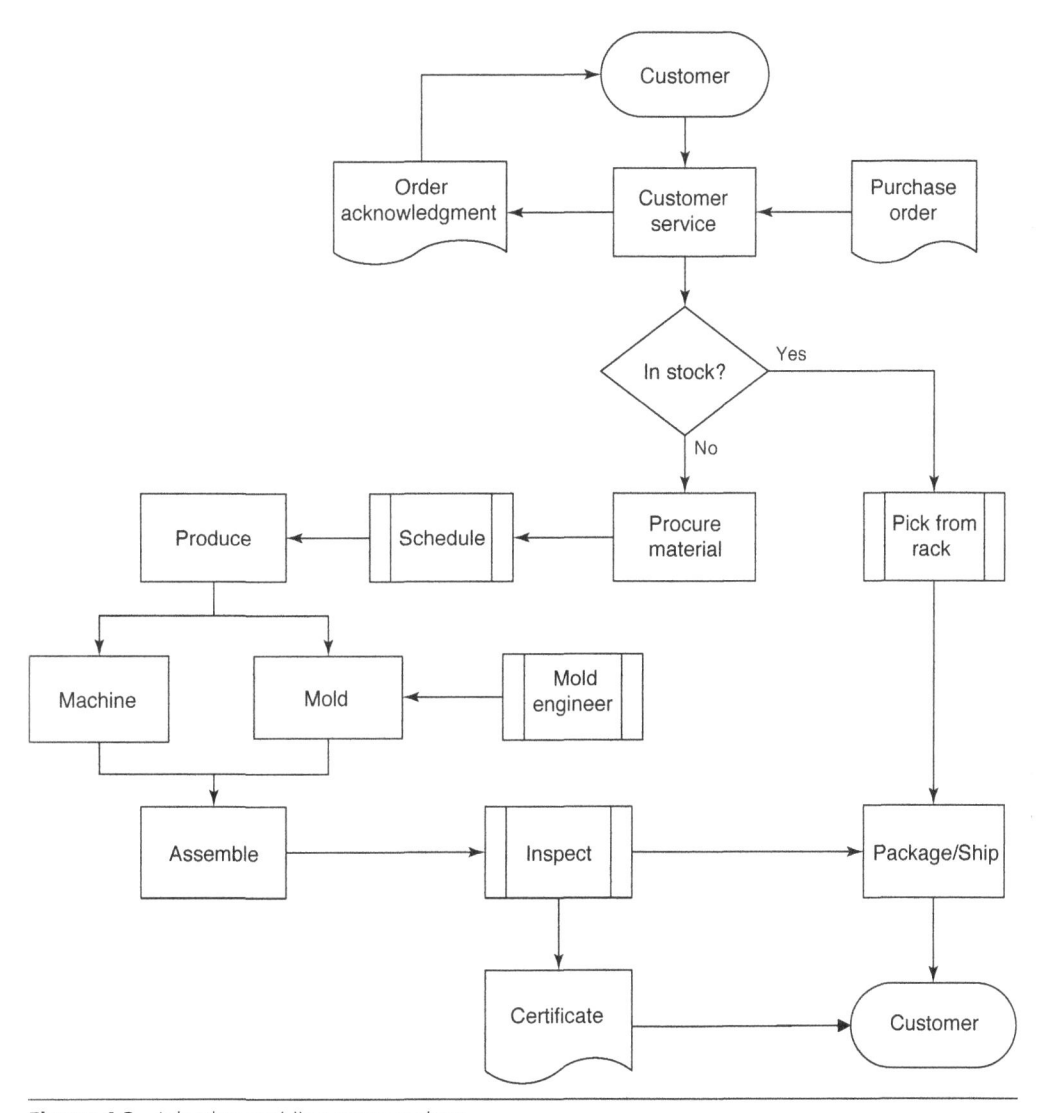

Figure 4.3 Injection molding process chart.

Many third-party auditors would not accept this description of the sequence and interaction of the processes, as it is not a graphical depiction of how the various processes interact. Some auditors would issue a nonconformance; others would coach the organization into adding a generic flowchart similar to the one shown in Figure 4.2. I contend that the generic chart provides *less* information than the written description. I would accept the Jones Plastics Company description *provided they had a process to control the interaction of the customer-oriented processes.*

Clause 4.1 of ISO 9001:2008 required the organization to "determine criteria and methods needed to ensure that both the operation and control of these processes are effective." Neither Figure 4.2 nor Figure 4.3 provides any evidence that the processes are under control. The sequence and interactions of the processes will be controlled as part of the organization's change control process. A change control process used by many organizations is the engineering change notice (ECN), which manages how processes interact. In the case of the Jones Plastics Company, if the purchasing department found a replacement for the supplier of resin, an ECN would be prepared so all other departments impacted by the change could review and approve it to ensure customer quality was maintained. Chapter 8 will provide more detail on change control requirements.

The ECN process *controls the interactions among the various processes*, which obviously has more value in meeting customer requirements than a flowchart depicting how the processes interact. However, a properly constructed flowchart can be a useful tool. If the Jones Plastics Company elected to use the injection molding process chart from Figure 4.3, in addition to satisfying the requirements of ISO 9001:2015, they would have an effective way of training new employees on how the various departments connect to produce the product. Additionally, the flowchart can assist internal auditors in indicating where quality records are required. In the chart in Figure 4.3, each customer order should have a record related to customer purchase order, order acknowledgment, and certificate of conformance.

Many organizations use flowcharts as a replacement for written procedures. While ISO 9001:2015 does not require the use of flowcharts, it strongly infers that organizations should understand process management:

> Clause 4.4.1: The organization shall determine the inputs and outputs expected from the processes needed for the quality management system and their application throughout the organization.

Management of processes such as sales/order entry, design, purchasing, and production can benefit when their procedures are mapped as a flowchart. Chapter 8 includes flowcharts to describe the design, sales, production, and service processes.

Note: Organizations often combine the interaction of support processes and the customer (or core) processes. For example, in Figure 4.4, if the product fails

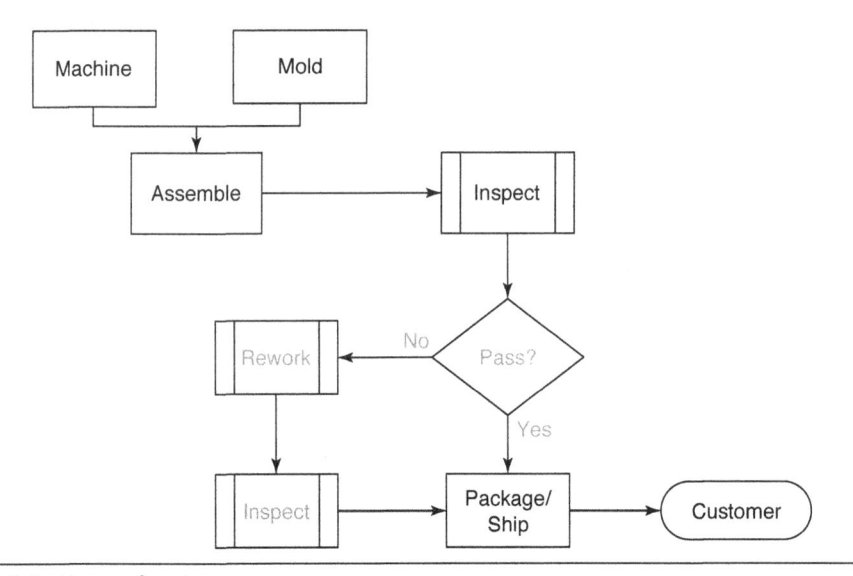

Figure 4.4 Nonconforming process.

at inspection, the control of nonconforming product can be added to the overall flowchart.

I don't feel that including support processes in the overall core process flowchart adds much value; in fact, in most cases where this is done, the flowchart becomes overly detailed and difficult to read. Each support process can be flowcharted, as will be illustrated in chapters 7, 9, and 10.

Audit Questions

Clause 4.4

What are the processes needed for the QMS and their application throughout the organization?

Examples: Marketing/sales, design/development, manufacturing, services, purchasing, engineering support, human resources, facilities, maintenance, quality assurance

How does the organization describe the inputs and outputs of the processes within the organization's scope of activities—including the interactions between the processes of the QMS?

Examples: Flowchart, description of processes

How are the interactions among the various processes controlled to ensure that customer requirements are met?

Example: Change control process

5
Clause 5: Leadership

#	ISO 9001:2015	#	ISO 9001:2008
5	Leadership	5	Management responsibility
5.1	Leadership and commitment	5.1	Management commitment
5.1.1	General	5.1	Management commitment
5.1.2	Customer focus	5.2	Customer focus
5.2	Policy	5.3	Quality policy
5.2.1	Establishing the quality policy	5.3	Quality policy
5.2.2	Communicating the quality policy	5.3	Quality policy
5.3	Organizational roles, responsibilities and authorities	5.5.1	Responsibility and authority

5.1 LEADERSHIP AND COMMITMENT

5.1.1 General

Top management shall demonstrate leadership and commitment with respect to the quality management system by taking accountability for the effectiveness of the quality management system. Top management shall:

- **Ensure the integration of the quality management system requirements into the organization's business processes;**
- **Promote the use of the process approach and risk-based thinking;**
- Ensure the resources needed for the quality management system are available;
- Communicate the importance of conforming to the quality management system requirements;
- Ensure that the quality management system achieves its intended results;
- Engage, direct and support the employees who contribute to the effectiveness of the quality management system;
- Promote improvement;
- Support all relevant management roles that apply to their areas of responsibility.

> **5.1.2 Customer focus**
>
> Top management shall demonstrate leadership and commitment with respect to customer focus by ensuring that customer and applicable statutory and regulatory requirements are determined and understood. Top management shall:
>
> - **Ensure the risks and opportunities that can affect conformity of products and services and the ability to enhance customer satisfaction are determined and addressed;**
> - Ensure the focus on enhancing customer satisfaction is maintained.

Clause 5.1.1 has the same requirements as ISO 9001:2008 clause 5.1, Management commitment, with the exception of the integration of the QMS requirements into the organization's business processes and the previously mentioned risk-based thinking.

Many ISO 9001–certified companies have integrated the QMS into their business planning and strategy. Companies of all sizes have woven the quality performance metrics into their business plan. Key performance indicators (KPIs) are assigned to quality and business parameters along with safety and environmental metrics. Quality-driven waste reduction projects include improved environmental performance. Best-in-class organizations have established a BMS combining their financial, quality, safety, and environmental systems into a cohesive operational model. Some ISO 9001–certified companies, however, operate with their QMS at arm's length from their business—just doing the minimum in ISO management to maintain certification. The ISO 9001:2015 requirements should nudge these companies into broadening their perspective on creating an integrated business management system.

Clause 5.1.2 is essentially the same as ISO 9001:2008 clause 5.2, Customer focus. Clause 5.1.2 places the responsibility on top management to ensure that statutory and regulatory requirements applicable to the product and customer satisfaction are met, as well as the new requirement of risk management.

> **Audit Questions**
>
> **Clause 5.1**
>
> The third-party auditors will interview top management at the site to assess their leadership and commitment as well as customer focus. The auditor may combine the assessment of leadership with the audit of the organization's management review process. Some questions that may be appropriate:
>
> *How does top management integrate the QMS requirements into the organization's business processes?*
>
> *What is the evidence to indicate that top management provides resources to support the QMS?*
>
> Examples: New equipment, resources
>
> *How does top management promote the use of the process approach and risk-based thinking?*

> *How does top management communicate the importance of effective quality management and of conformance to the QMS requirements?*
>
> *How does top management demonstrate leadership and commitment with respect to customer focus by ensuring that customer requirements and applicable statutory and regulatory requirements are determined, understood, and consistently met?*
>
> *How does top management assess the risks and opportunities that can affect conformity of products and services?*

5.2 POLICY

> ### 5.2.1 Establishing the quality policy
>
> **Top management shall establish, implement and maintain a quality policy that is appropriate to the purpose and context of the organization and supports its strategic direction.**
> The quality policy shall:
>
> - Provide a framework for setting quality objectives;
> - Include a commitment to satisfy applicable requirements;
> - Include a commitment to continually improve the quality management system.
>
> ### 5.2.2 Communicating the quality policy
>
> The quality policy shall be available and maintained as documented information and be communicated, understood and applied within the organization.
> The quality policy shall be available to relevant interested parties, as appropriate.

The quality policy requirement in ISO 9001:2015 is essentially the same as ISO 9001:2008 with the exception of the addition of "context of the organization and supports its strategic direction." The *context* and *strategic direction* considerations are overarching requirements of ISO 9001:2015. In reference to the quality policy, they present an opportunity for the organization to evaluate how its quality policy relates to the overall business model of the company.

A common area of confusion is how to communicate the quality policy to employees when the company also has a mission statement and a vision. What's the difference between a vision, a mission, and a quality policy? Generally, they are defined as follows:

Vision. What the organization aspires to be. How the future will look if the organization achieves its mission.

Mission. What the organization is all about. Who we are, who our customers are, what we do, and how we do it.

Quality policy. A guide as to how the organization should provide products and services to customers.

In the case of the Jones Plastics Company, the company established the following vision statement, mission statement, and quality policy:

Vision Statement

The Jones Plastics Company will be the injection molding manufacturer of choice.

Mission Statement

The Jones Plastics Company will:

- Innovatively manufacture injection-molded products to the highest quality standards

- Provide superior service and application technology to our customers and maintain a cooperative partnership with our suppliers

- Create a challenging, rewarding, and safe working environment for our employees

- Be recognized as a good corporate citizen, conducting business in accordance with the highest ethical standards while providing profits satisfactory to our stockholders

Quality Policy

The Jones Plastics Company will satisfy the needs and expectations of our customers by understanding their requirements and providing high-quality products that meet or exceed all performance requirements, while promoting full employee involvement and empowerment.

The Jones Plastics Company quality policy appears to be appropriate to the purpose and context of the organization and supports its strategic direction, as it is consistent with the mission and vision statements. It includes "a commitment to satisfy applicable requirements" and a commitment to continual improvement ("exceed all performance requirements"). Does the Jones Plastics Company's Quality Policy "provide a framework for setting quality objectives"?

As a third-party auditor, I would challenge the Jones Plastics Company to show me the objectives that support "high-quality" and "exceed all performance requirements." If the company's rate of rejection from their customers approached zero defect levels and their customers provided very positive testimonials (customer feedback), then I would congratulate them. I would also want to explore examples of how the employees were empowered and involved. Employee improvement teams, implemented suggestions, employee satisfaction surveys, positive employee interviews—all could demonstrate that the Jones Plastics Company was committed to employee empowerment.

In this type of objectives review, an experienced auditor would be judicious in responding to organizations that overcommitted in their quality policy without hard evidence supporting their policy, especially related to exceeding requirements. It is generally better for the organization to use *expectations* rather than *requirement*s, as expectations are more subjective and can be supported by positive customer feedback. Many organizations want to instill a culture of excellence among their employees—they don't want to just meet requirements, as that is only being "good enough." I would not recommend that an organization like the Jones Plastics Company rewrite their quality policy unless their quality performance was well below high quality. I would challenge them to spend some time analyzing options to provide some measures supporting the claims in their policy.

One of the more challenging situations for an auditor representing a registrar is auditing a client for the first time and observing a quality policy that is more like a bumper sticker or vision statement, with outlandish, unsupported high-quality claims—and realizing it had been approved for several years by auditors from the same registrar. Several years ago, I was auditing with a team member who chose to push the client (auditee) into changing certain parts of the company's documentation. The client threw the quality procedures manual across the room. "The auditor from your company had me change the documentation last year—now you want me to change it back?" he exclaimed, rather loudly.

Very early in my auditing career, I challenged the president of a Fortune 500 fiber optics company on their quality policy. "We anticipate our customer's needs and provide leading-edge solutions"—truly a mismatch with the concept of a quality policy. The policy had been approved by the previous auditors for several years. That was the only client in my 20 years of auditing that requested I not be assigned to them again. After that experience, I decided there are many real issues that impact a client's quality performance that I should focus on, and that debating semantics on a quality policy is probably not one of them. That fiber optics company would deliver the same quality products to their customers whether they had a "proper" policy or not.

The overarching requirement of ISO 9001:2015 is to integrate the QMS into the company's business model. I suggest organizations review their quality policy for consistency with their business strategy—their vision and mission—and find ways to clearly communicate the quality policy to employees.

Audit Questions

Clause 5.2

Does the policy:
- Provide a framework for setting quality objectives?
- Include a commitment to satisfy applicable requirements?
- Include a commitment to the continual improvement of the QMS?

Is the quality policy appropriate to the purpose and context of the organization, and does it support its strategic direction?

How is the quality policy communicated to employees? Temporary help? Contractors?

How is the quality policy made available to the public or interested parties?

5.3 ORGANIZATIONAL ROLES, RESPONSIBILITIES AND AUTHORITIES

> Top management shall ensure that the responsibilities and authorities for relevant roles are assigned and communicated within the organization. Top management shall assign the responsibility and authority for:
>
> - Ensuring that the quality management system conforms to the requirements of this International Standard;
> - Ensuring the processes are delivering their intended outputs;
> - Reporting on the performance of the quality management system and on opportunities for improvement to top management;
> - Ensuring the promotion of customer focus throughout the organization;
> - Ensuring that the integrity of the quality management system is maintained when changes to the quality management system are planned and implemented.

Top management should assign responsibilities and authorities to ensure the QMS is maintained. The organization's documented information should define individual responsibility and authority for maintaining the QMS.

What's new compared to ISO 9001:2008? The **ISO 9001:2015** standard does not use the title "management representative" as previous ISO 9001 standards did. However, the organization can continue to use this title to convey certain responsibilities. The intent of ISO 9001:2015 is to emphasize top management's responsibilities as going beyond delegating.

In my past experiences with a small group of organizations, management had delegated the quality management coordination too far down the organizational chart. This was evident when the quality management representative did not attend the management review meetings to present the status of the QMS—not a good sign. Management's explanation for this was that financial and other sensitive issues needed to be discussed at the meeting, and the quality coordinator should not be privy to such information. Organizations exhibiting such traits usually had a very weak business plan and QMS. ISO 9001:2015 attempts to prevent the overdelegation of QMS management.

It is important to understand the difference between authority and responsibility. In the business context, *responsibility* is the obligation of a subordinate to perform a duty as required by his or her supervisor. The person accepting responsibility is accountable for the performance of the assigned duties. *Authority* is the power assigned to an executive or a manager in order to achieve certain organizational objectives. Clause 5.3 requires that the organization be clear on who is authorized to approve changes to customer purchase orders, product for shipment to customers, deviations from approved specifications or drawings, the release of reworked product, machine process parameters, and new suppliers.

While the designation of authorities and assignment of responsibilities appears trite, ISO 9001 auditors often encounter situations where changes in instructions occur rather haphazardly, sometimes without any approval. For organizations building a QMS or rebuilding one, I suggest including documented information that clearly defines what job titles have the authorities of approval to manage the business and what job titles will be responsible for executing the various tasks. Chapter 6 will review change control.

> **Audit Questions**
>
> **Clause 5.3**
>
> *How has the organization determined:*
>
> - Authorities?
> - Responsibilities?
>
> *What individual (title) has the responsibility to:*
>
> - Report to top management on the performance of the QMS and on opportunities for improvement?
> - Ensure the promotion of customer focus throughout the organization?
> - Ensure that the integrity of the QMS is maintained when changes to the QMS are planned and implemented?
>
> *Who has the authority to approve:*
>
> - Changes to customer purchase orders?
> - Product for shipment to customers?
> - Deviations from approved specifications or drawings?
> - Release of reworked product?
> - Machine process parameters?
> - New suppliers?

6
Clause 6: Planning

#	ISO 9001:2015	#	ISO 9001:2008
6	Planning	5.4	Planning
6.1	Actions to address risks and opportunities	—	NEW
6.2	Quality objectives and planning to achieve them	5.4.1	Quality objectives
6.3	Planning of changes	5.4.2	Quality management system planning

6.1 ACTIONS TO ADDRESS RISKS AND OPPORTUNITIES

> **6.1.1:** When planning for the quality management system, the organization shall consider the context of the organization and the needs of interested parties.
> The organization shall determine the risks and opportunities that need to be addressed to give assurance that the quality management system can:
>
> - Achieve its intended results;
> - Enhance desirable effects;
> - Prevent, or reduce, undesired effects;
> - Achieve improvement.
>
> **6.1.2:** The organization shall plan:
>
> - Actions to address these risks and opportunities;
> - How to integrate and implement the actions into its quality management system processes;
> - How to evaluate the effectiveness of these actions.
>
> Actions taken to address risks and opportunities shall be proportionate to the potential impact on the conformity of products and services.

The requirement to provide risk analysis in QMS activities is a key difference in **ISO 9001:2015** compared to previous revisions. The organization is now required to assess the risks and opportunities related to its purpose, its business strategy, and the expectations of interested parties to ensure the QMS meets its objectives. Quality tools currently used in many organizations include strategic planning process, SWOT analysis, Six Sigma, and lean manufacturing programs. Results of the analysis should be used in establishing objectives and planning to mitigate the risks. FMEA could be used. While organizations with an effective QMS certainly understand the risks related to their operations, the new requirements of ISO 9001:2015 may have a positive effect on many organizations by requiring a more formalized risk evaluation process and subjecting it to a third-party audit. It should be noted that ISO 9001:2015 does not have a requirement for preventive action. The reasoning is that the entire QMS is preventive in nature, as is the risk analysis approach. Organizations may believe that the preventive actions they have used for several years provide risk analysis appropriate to their business. I can imagine a discussion between a third-party auditor and the quality manager of a small machine shop:

Auditor: You are no longer required to use preventive actions. What is your process for risk management?

Auditee: For over 10 years, you have harangued me, gigged me, and coached me on preventive actions. Now that I finally understand the difference between corrective and preventive actions, you say I don't need PA! My risk analysis process is our preventive actions. Want to see our five PAs for this year?

Auditor: Let me check with my registrar's office.

In this case, I would suggest the auditor accept the preventive actions as a risk analysis approach, provided the actions will reduce or eliminate the probability of specific undesirable events from happening in the future—and not just prevent a corrective action situation from reoccurring. The organization should be encouraged to avail itself of other options for risk analysis.

For many organizations, the use of design and process FMEAs can be an effective tool to assure the QMS can achieve its intended results and satisfy ISO 9001:2015 requirements for risk analysis. The American Society for Quality (ASQ) website provides guidance on when and how to use the FMEA process (http://asq.org/learn-about-quality/process-analysis-tools/overview/fmea.html). See Appendix B for a FMEA summary. ASQ suggests when to use FMEA:

- When a process, product, or service is being designed or redesigned, after quality function deployment
- When an existing process, product, or service is being applied in a new way
- Before developing control plans for a new or modified process
- When improvement goals are planned for an existing process, product, or service
- When analyzing failures of an existing process, product, or service
- Periodically throughout the life of the process, product, or service

One of my more interesting auditing clients was a large manufacturer of semiconductors and microprocessor chips. Semiconductor material manufacturers are quite complex and also difficult to audit. The processes take place in a clean-room environment, where all visitors (including auditors) have to wear the same uniforms and face masks as the employees to keep dirt away from the product.

Auditors are required to use special fiber-free paper to take notes. It takes about two tours of this type of site to start to understand the processes and provide value to the client. On my third audit, the quality manager asked me to focus on their change control process as part of my audit plan. ISO 9001:2008 had the following requirements related to changes:

> 4.2.3 *Control of documents:* A documented procedure shall be established to define the controls needed to ensure that changes and the current revision status of documents are identified.
>
> 5.4.2 *Quality management system planning:* Top management shall ensure that: b) the integrity of the quality management system is maintained when changes to the quality management system are planned and implemented.

When auditing to the requirements of clause 4.2.3, occasionally lapses are found in an organization's system that allow some obsolete documents to remain in use. The risks related to changes in the QMS can be an issue when the organization adds new equipment to the site and fails to include the equipment on the maintenance schedule. These areas, especially document control, maintenance, and calibration, are usually fertile ground for the organization's internal auditors—and frankly do not present a major risk to the company's quality performance. What the quality manager was looking for were changes in materials or processes that could slip by their change control system—resulting in a major rejection of very expensive product at various steps in the process. The company had apparently experienced such an event.

On this audit, I decided to dig deeper than I normally would into raw material approval and specification changes. In the purchasing department, I sampled the purchase orders for several chemicals recently used in making the chips. I recorded the supplier's specification number and revision from the purchase order. Next, the receiving department was sampled to match the certificate of analysis (COA) for that material. In 2 cases out of the 10 sampled, the COA included specifications for the chemical's parameters that did not match the supplier's specification on file with the quality department. While the discrepancies were not a major risk, the quality manager recognized the gap in their raw material approval process. A bigger issue was the inconsistency in signing off on the COAs: Some technicians would initial and date the COA, and others would not. I suggested three improvements:

- Update the raw material receiving procedure to require the initialing and dating of COAs
- Retrain the technicians on the updated procedure
- Conduct an internal audit of all critical raw materials: COA vs. supplier specifications

From that point on in my auditing career, I found that many companies were at risk related to maintaining up-to-date specifications. Often, familiarity breeds complacency in the quality inspection world. Many large chemical suppliers modify specifications or manufacturing processes without notifying their customers, since they believe the change is an improvement and will not impact the chemical's performance. Depending on the organization's operations, I suggest that changes related to controlling raw materials be a priority in risk management.

I also recommend that organizations carefully review the pros and cons of establishing a risk-based thinking initiative in their organization. My observations on risk-based thinking follow.

Risk-Based Thinking

The release of ISO 9001:2015 has triggered considerable interest in the application of risk-based thinking in the quality management field.[1] A common tool or technique employed in risk-based thinking is the use of a risk register or log. While there are many variants on a risk register, the key elements are similar to those of a process FMEA and usually include:

- Description of the risk
- Risk type (business, quality, design)
- Likelihood of occurrence
- Severity
- Countermeasures
- Process owner
- Status/updates

The likelihood of occurrence and severity calculations use ranking criteria to help prioritize the countermeasures and actions to mitigate the risk.

While risk-based thinking can be valuable in assisting the organization in managing risks and improving their QMS (and complying to ISO 9001:2015 requirements), I have concerns that risk-based thinking implemented as a *cultural* change for organizations will not be very successful. In the past 30 years, there have been several quality improvement initiatives that attempted to bring about a change in a company's culture but did not have a sustainable impact on the company's quality or business results. Noted examples include:

- Quality circles in the 1970s
- Total quality management (TQM) in the 1980s
- Business process reengineering (BPR) in the 1990s

While each of these programs had successes, a common reason for their lack of sustainability was the failure of the programs to become part of the day-to-day functioning of the business. Unfortunately, the programs were often seen as management's latest fad. In my work life, I have had the opportunity to work with all three of these programs.

Quality circles were often unsuccessful because members of the group lacked the power or skills to change the existing company work structure or procedures. At a circle I was involved with at the Polaroid Corporation, the manufacturing

---

1. For readers interested in pursuing risk-based thinking as applied to ISO 9001:2015, ASQ has a list of training opportunities and books at http://asq.org/training/Risk-Management-Essentials-and-Implementation-strategies_RMEIS.html.

machine operators would generate ideas to improve the process, but they lacked the skills to implement the changes, which were often machinery upgrades. Management did not assign mechanics or engineers to be part of the circle. In a few months, the circle members became frustrated and the teams were disbanded.

TQM teams also often failed due to a lack of management commitment. According to Rosabeth Moss Kanter of Harvard Business School:

> When TQM efforts fail, it is because they are mounted as programs, unconnected to business strategy, rigidly and narrowly applied, and expected to bring about miraculous transformations in the short term without management lifting as much as a finger. (Quoted in Balestracci 2009)

At Polaroid in the early 1990s, a few years prior to its bankruptcy, there were as many as 50 total quality ownership (TQO) teams functioning throughout the company. (Polaroid replaced "management" with "ownership" in support of its employee stock ownership plan.) While Polaroid's management invested in employee training and time away from the team member's jobs, the output of the TQO teams contributed little to Polaroid's results. As indicated in the quote by Rosabeth Moss Kanter, the TQO initiatives were not closely connected to the company's business strategy. Total quality ownership (or management) can improve product quality or efficiency; it cannot invent new products.

BPR often failed because of existing company culture. In their book *Reengineering the Corporation: A Manifesto for Business Revolution*, James Champy and Michael Hammer state:

> A company's prevailing cultural characteristics can inhibit or defeat a reengineering effort before it begins. For instance, if a company operates by consensus, its people will find the top-down nature of reengineering an affront to their sensibilities. Companies whose short-term orientations keep them exclusively focused on quarterly results may find it difficult to extend their vision to reengineering's longer horizons. Organizations with a bias against conflict may be uncomfortable challenging long-established rules. It is executive management's responsibility to anticipate and overcome such barriers. (Champy and Hammer 1993, 207)

Polaroid invested heavily in BPR in an attempt to improve operating efficiency and time-to-market for new products. I attended seminars conducted by BPR founder Michael Hammer and was part of a company-wide program to reengineer the packaging of Polaroid instant film products. The BPR programs appeared to have support from senior management, but middle management had little motivation to change the processes that had kept them nicely rewarded for many years.

Quality managers planning to establish risk-based thinking as a new *culture* in their company as part of implementing ISO 9001:2015 may want to review the failures of the programs listed above. Before embarking on risk-based thinking, quality managers should ensure that both top management and middle managers are on board and committed to supporting and implementing this new thought process. Quality initiatives that have been successful in the last several years are Six Sigma and lean manufacturing (discussed in Chapter 10). In my opinion, the reason these programs have achieved success is that while they do include some level of culture change for the organization's employees—or different thought processes—they are also results driven. Top management support is important, but middle managers and work staff can operate quite independently and effectively once they are provided a charter by management for a Six Sigma or lean initiative.

I recommend that quality managers seeking to initiate risk-based thinking in their organization consider employing risk *analysis* specific to the organization's processes. The *Handbook* points out several areas where risk analysis should be employed:

- *Process or equipment changes: Chapter 6.* When production equipment or processes are changed, the implementation plan should include the potential risk to product quality. Testing a "new" material product prior to release to customers is a common technique employed, along with the application of FMEA.

- *Raw material specification control: Chapter 6.* Any change in materials used in production should be tested before release to customers. The organization should ensure its suppliers are aware of the need to communicate and maintain control of any changes in their specifications or processes.

- *Document control and review: Chapter 7.* The organization should ensure that documents used by employees are maintained and controlled to avoid mistakes. Employee instructions should be reviewed at some frequency to ensure employees are not bypassing operating instructions.

- *Design: Chapter 8.* During the design process, a robust verification and validation plan should be employed to eliminate risks related to new designs. The new design process should also include a risk analysis related to the impact the new design process may have on employee safety and the environment, including end-of-life disposal issues.

- *Regulatory updates: Chapter 8.* The organization should maintain a process to stay up to date on changes to statutory and regulatory obligations related to its products to eliminate risks related to noncompliance.

- *Outsourced processes: Chapter 8.* Processes performed by external parties can create a risk for the organization in meeting its commitment. External supplier selection should include controls related to the impact the supplier could have on producing acceptable products or services. Inspection of externally supplied products should be based on inspection cost versus risk related to supplier errors.

- *Planning of internal audits: Chapter 9.* The timing of internal audits for various processes should be based on the impact the process has on quality performance as well as the history the particular process has of generating nonconformances. By focusing on the history and impact of each process, the organization can allocate auditing resources to reduce the risk of errors.

- *Effectiveness of corrective actions: Chapter 10.* An important consideration in the corrective action process is how effectively the correction reduces the risk of the same issue recurring. Time and resources allocated to measuring the effectiveness of the correction should be commensurate with the risk of recurrence.

> **Audit Questions**
>
> **Clause 6.1**
>
> *How does the organization assess the risks and opportunities related to its purpose, its business strategy, and the expectations of interested parties to ensure the QMS meets its objectives?*
>
> Examples: Strategic planning process, SWOT analysis, Six Sigma, lean manufacturing
>
> *What are some examples of how the organization addresses the identified risks and opportunities?*
>
> Examples: Reports or records of risk analysis

6.2 QUALITY OBJECTIVES AND PLANNING TO ACHIEVE THEM

> 6.2.1: The organization shall establish quality objectives at relevant functions, levels and processes needed for the quality management system.
>
> The quality objectives shall:
>
> - Be consistent with the quality policy;
> - Be measurable;
> - Take into account applicable requirements;
> - Be relevant to conformity of products and services to enhancement of customer satisfaction;
> - Be monitored; be communicated; be updated as appropriate.
>
> The organization shall maintain documented information on the quality objectives.
>
> **6.2.2: When planning how to achieve its quality objectives, the organization shall determine:**
>
> - **What will be done; what resources will be required;**
> - **Who will be responsible;**
> - **When it will be completed;** how the results will be evaluated.

New to **ISO 9001:2015** is the more direct statement requiring the organization to establish programs to implement quality objectives. ISO 9001:2008 clause 5.4.1, Quality objectives, states:

> Top management shall ensure that quality objectives, including those needed to meet requirements for product, are established at relevant functions and levels within the organization. The quality objectives shall be measurable and consistent with the quality policy.

The planning required to implement the quality objectives was somewhat vague. While past revisions of ISO 9001 gave organizations some flexibility in implementing their quality objectives, third-party auditors will now expect the organization to have a defined program to achieve each of its quality objectives. This requirement is consistent with ISO 14001:2015 and should reduce auditing inconsistencies—and enhance quality improvements.

Audit Questions

Clause 6.2

Are the quality objectives consistent with the quality policy?

Are the quality objectives measurable?

Are the quality objectives relevant to product or service conformity?

How does the organization communicate the quality objectives to employees?

In planning to achieve the quality objectives, does the organization establish:

- What will be done?
- What resources will be required?
- Who will be responsible?
- When it will be completed?
- How the results will be evaluated?

How are the quality objectives monitored, and what actions are taken when the objectives are not met?

6.3 PLANNING OF CHANGES

When the organization determines the need for changes to the quality management system, the changes shall be carried out in a planned manner. The organization shall consider:

- The purpose of the changes and their potential consequences;
- The integrity of the quality management system;
- The availability of resources;
- The allocation or reallocation of responsibilities and authorities.

Clause 6.3 is very similar to ISO 9001:2008 clause 5.4.2, Quality management system planning, which states:

> Top management shall ensure that the integrity of the quality management system is maintained when changes to the quality management system are planned and implemented.

As described under clause 6.1, Actions to address risks and opportunities, changes in the QMS can represent a threat to the organization's performance. An effective change control process will include a cross-functional sign-off on changes in the manufacturing or service processes. The ECN or similar system will require that the appropriate individuals review and approve changes to ensure product quality is maintained when changes occur. Changes to customer or supplier specifications, deviations from approved specifications or drawings, changes in machine process parameters, and qualifying new suppliers are all examples of where multidepartment sign-off should be employed.

At Polaroid I witnessed (and survived) several situations where change control was inadequate, even though the company had a process in place. Polaroid's instant film cassette included a six-volt flat battery to power the camera's flash system and electronics. The battery had thin aluminum collector plates (anode and cathode) that required a conductive adhesive to connect the cells of the battery. The purchasing department, under pressure to cut costs, challenged the aluminum supplier (a Fortune 500 company) to reduce the cost by 10%. To accomplish this goal, the aluminum supplier reduced the number of passes through the rolling mill, which lowered labor costs. Each pass through the mill now consumed too much energy, so the aluminum company changed the type of lubricant it used. The aluminum company did not disclose the lubricant change because they felt it would not affect the finished collector plates.

Several million dollars' worth of batteries and film had to be scrapped a few months later. The new lubricant on the aluminum interacted with the conductive adhesive, causing the flat battery to delaminate—not immediately, but a few months after assembly. Polaroid's change control process had been followed. The key issue was the aluminum supplier's failure to disclose the change in lubricant (they later claimed it was a proprietary formula). One of the learning points after the fiasco was to strengthen Polaroid's supplier agreements to restrict material substitution or process changes without Polaroid's approval.

I include this example to show that failures in manufacturing can be caused by *culture* as much as a lack of discipline and controls. In the Polaroid aluminum scenario, the massive failure could have been avoided if a few warning signs had not been dismissed. In the first qualification trial of the aluminum, the test and control performed exactly the same—but only because the test engineer mislabeled the materials, and the test and control were actually from the same lot of standard material. The purchasing manager was hell-bent on implementing the cost savings (perhaps his bonus was in play?), so he convinced the technical manager to bypass the usual repeat trials of new material. A young engineer noted that the first run of the new aluminum did not laminate as well as the standard material ("What does *she* know?" was the technical manager's response). I collected all this information to convince Polaroid's president that the battery plant had sufficiently improved our change control process to avoid a repeat of the aluminum problem. He left me with this advice: "When making changes in materials in the future, instead of proving why the change is going to be successful, assume that it will *not work*—and develop a plan to prove it does. With that approach you will not be as apt to miss signals."

Audit Question

Clause 6.3

What process does the organization use to ensure that changes in processes, products, and services do not have an adverse effect on the integrity of the organization's QMS?

Examples of areas where organizations may be at risk when changes occur:

- Materials—suppliers
- Product specifications
- Process or equipment settings
- Customer design
- Regulatory requirements

7
Clause 7: Support

#	ISO 9001:2015	#	ISO 9001:2008
7	Support	6	Resource management
7.1	Resources	5.1	Management commitment
7.1.1	General	6.1	Provision of resources
7.1.2	People	5.1	Management commitment
7.1.3	Infrastructure	6.3	Infrastructure
7.1.4	Environment for the operation of processes	6.4	Work environment
7.1.5	Monitoring and measuring resources	7.6	Control of monitoring and measuring equipment
7.1.6	Organizational knowledge	—	NEW
7.2	Competence	6.2.2	Competence, training and awareness
7.3	Awareness	6.2.2	Competence, training and awareness
7.4	Communication	5.5.3	Internal communication
7.5	Documented information	4.2	Documentation requirements
7.5.1	General	4.2	Documentation requirements
7.5.2	Creating and updating	4.2.3	Control of documents
7.5.3	Control of documented information	4.2.3	Control of documents
		4.2.4	Control of records

Clause 7 groups several clauses of ISO 9001:2008 into one major clause: Support. This change allows for alignment with ISO 14001:2015. New to **ISO 9001:2015** is clause 7.1.6, Organizational knowledge. Figure 7.1 groups the subclauses of clause 7.

```
                          ┌─────────────┐
                          │     7       │
                          │  Support    │
                          └──────┬──────┘
          ┌──────────┬──────────┼──────────┬──────────┐
          ▼          ▼          ▼          ▼          ▼
      ┌───────┐  ┌───────┐  ┌───────┐  ┌────────────┐  ┌──────────────┐
      │ 7.1   │  │ 7.2   │  │ 7.3   │  │ 7.4        │  │ 7.5          │
      │Resources│ │Competence│ │Awareness│ │Communication│ │Documentation│
      └───────┘  └───────┘  └───────┘  └────────────┘  └──────────────┘
```

7.1.1 General
7.1.2 People
7.1.3 Infrastructure
7.1.4 Environment
7.1.5 Monitoring
7.1.6 Organizational knowledge

7.5.1 General
7.5.2 Creating
7.5.3 Control

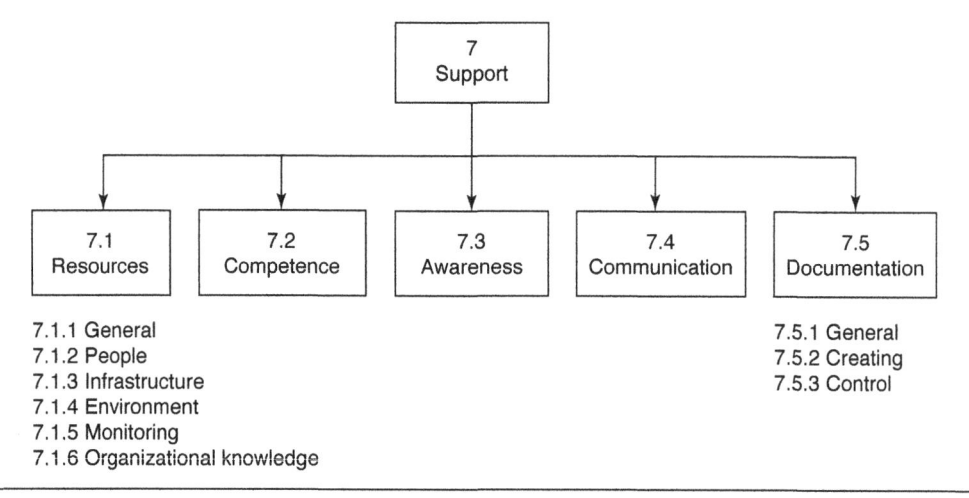

Figure 7.1 Clause 7: Support.

7.1 RESOURCES

7.1.1 General

The organization shall determine and provide the resources needed for the establishment, implementation, maintenance and continual improvement of the quality management system, considering the capabilities of existing internal resources and what needs to be obtained from external providers.

7.1.2 People

The organization shall determine and provide the persons necessary for the effective implementation of its quality management system and for the operation and control of its processes.

7.1.3 Infrastructure

The organization shall determine, provide and maintain the infrastructure necessary for the operation of its processes and to achieve conformity of products and services.

7.1.4 Environment for the operation of processes

The organization shall determine, provide and maintain the environment necessary for the operation of its processes and to achieve conformity of products and services.

7.1.5 Monitoring and measuring resources

7.1.5.1 General

The organization shall determine and provide the resources needed to ensure valid and reliable results when monitoring or measuring is used to verify the conformity of products and services to requirements.

7.1.5.2 Measurement traceability

When measurement traceability is a requirement, or is considered by the organization to be an essential part of providing confidence in the validity of measurement results, measuring equipment shall be:

- Calibrated or verified, or both, at specified intervals, or prior to use, against measurement standards;
- Traceable to international or national measurement standards; when no such standards exist, the basis used for calibration or verification shall be retained as documented information;
- Identified in order to determine its status;
- Safeguarded from adjustments, damage or deterioration that would invalidate the calibration status and subsequent measurement results.

The organization shall determine if the validity of previous measurement results has been adversely affected when measuring equipment is found to be unfit for its intended purpose, and shall take appropriate action as necessary.

7.1.6 Organizational knowledge

The organization shall determine the knowledge necessary for the operation of its processes and to achieve conformity of products and services. When addressing changing needs and trends, the organization shall consider its current knowledge and determine how to acquire or access any necessary additional knowledge and required updates.

Clause 7.1 defining the requirements for resources is essentially the same as existing clauses in ISO 9001:2008, except for the new subclause, 7.1.6.

While ISO 9001:2008 clause 6.2.1, Human resources—General ("Personnel performing work affecting conformity to product requirements shall be competent on the basis of appropriate education, training, skills and experience"), implied that organizations should maintain organizational knowledge, ISO 9001:2015 requires that organizations consider and review their processes to ensure that operational/process or product knowledge is maintained when employees leave the organization, and to review processes used by the organization to remain knowledgeable about new technology relevant to its business model.

The key phrase in the new organizational knowledge clause is "consider its current knowledge." A third-party auditor would expect the organization, depending on its operations, to have some formalized program for succession planning, technology updates, and supplier contingencies. Many ISO 9001–certified organizations have processes in place for maintaining organizational knowledge by way of their business strategy and contingency plan. The organization's internal auditors and third-party auditors need to be sensitive to possible confidentiality issues with this information. Additionally, since the requirement is for the organization to *consider* its current knowledge and determine how to acquire or access any necessary additional knowledge, auditors should not require the organization to implement actions to acquire additional knowledge; the implementation of a business strategy is confidential and outside the scope of ISO 9001 and the skill set of the majority of ISO auditors.

Clause 7.1.3, Infrastructure, requires the organization to maintain facilities and support processes such as transport/trucking, information systems, accounting, production machine maintenance, and plant equipment such as air, vacuum, water, and steam sources. In most organizations, maintenance of machinery and facilities equipment has the biggest impact on the organization's quality performance. The older versions of ISO 9001 included the concept of maintaining *production machinery* in order to maintain *process capability*—still a good idea. Maintenance of computer-based support equipment can also be important, in the area of data backup. Some organizations find it helpful to measure the effectiveness of the preventive maintenance process by monitoring the percentage of time machines are available for production.

Clause 7.1.4, Environment for the operation of processes—formerly clause 6.4, Work environment—has been a source of confusion for both auditors and auditees. The writers of ISO 9001:2015 did not help resolve the situation. A note in clause 7.1.4 reads:

> A suitable environment can be a combination of human and physical factors, such as:
>
> a) Social (e.g. non-discriminatory, calm, non-confrontational);
>
> b) Psychological (e.g. stress-reducing, burnout prevention, emotionally protective);
>
> c) Physical (e.g. temperature, heat, humidity, light, airflow, hygiene, noise).
>
> These factors can differ substantially depending on the products and services provided.

Clause 7.1.4 requires the organization to determine, provide, and maintain the environment necessary for the operation of its processes and for achieving conformity of products and services. So, should the organization (and the auditor) be concerned that a nervous or sweaty employee will make a poor product? I believe that the intent of clause 7.1.4 is to cover work environment issues (e.g., work area temperature, humidity, electrostatic conditions, dirt) that can cause nonconforming product. Many products need to be produced (and measured) in a controlled temperature/humidity environment. Electronic circuit boards often must be produced in an atmosphere free of electrostatic charge from employees; similarly, many products need to be produced in an atmosphere free of dirt or other contamination. While organizations should maintain a safe and relatively clean and comfortable workplace, auditing to those requirements should not be in the scope of ISO 9001.

An auditor colleague of mine once remarked when observing some safety violations in a plant, "The organization won't meet its shipping commitments if OSHA puts a lock on the door!" This approach is not helpful. Quality auditors should focus on quality.

Clause 7.1.5.2, Measurement traceability, covers what was clause 7.6 in ISO 9001:2008, Control of monitoring and measuring equipment. There is no change in requirements. Most organizations refer to this process as calibration and have controls in place. I don't have official statistics on this, but my instincts tell me that when it comes to nonconformances issued by auditors, gaps in calibration probably rank at the top of the list. A well-maintained calibration process is part of the discipline ISO 9001 brings to companies of all sizes and levels of complexity.

Audit Questions

Clause 7.1.3

What are the supporting services in the scope of the QMS? How are they managed to support the QMS?

Examples: Transport/trucking, information systems, accounting, machine maintenance, plant equipment (air, vacuum, water, steam), powered lift truck maintenance

How is the effectiveness of the maintenance process measured or monitored?

Examples: Machine efficiency, machine downtime/uptime

Clause 7.1.4

What are the work environment conditions or parameters that could have an impact on product quality?

Examples: Temperature, humidity, electrostatic discharge, dirt/contamination

Clause 7.1.5.2

How does the organization ensure that its devices:

- Identify their calibration status?
- Are calibrated or verified at specified intervals?
- Are measured against traceable standards?
- Are adjusted or readjusted as necessary?
- Are safeguarded from adjustments?
- Are protected from damage and deterioration?

When the equipment or device is found not to conform to calibration requirements, what action does the organization take?

Clause 7.1.6

What process does the organization use to ensure operational/process or product knowledge is maintained when employees leave the organization?

What process is used by the organization to remain knowledgeable about new technology?

7.2 COMPETENCE

The organization shall determine the necessary competence of persons doing work under its control that affects the performance and effectiveness of the quality management system.
   The organization shall:

- Ensure that these persons are competent on the basis of appropriate education, training or experience;
- Where applicable, take actions to acquire the necessary competence, and evaluate the effectiveness of the actions taken;
- Retain appropriate documented information as evidence of competence.

7.3 AWARENESS

> The organization shall ensure that persons doing work under the organization's control are aware of:
>
> - The quality policy;
> - Relevant quality objectives;
> - Their contribution to the effectiveness of the quality management system, including the benefits of improved performance;
> - The implications of not conforming to the quality management system requirements.

7.4 COMMUNICATION

> The organization shall determine the internal and external communications relevant to the quality management system, including who will communicate, on what it will communicate, when to communicate and with whom to communicate.

ISO 9001:2015 has no new requirements for competence, awareness, or communication. Table 7.1 distinguishes the intent and conformance evidence among the three clauses.

There is no change in ISO 9001:2015 related to competence. The organization must identify the competence, skills, and training needed to support the QMS. Competence in the context of an industrial plant and as defined by ISO 9001:2015 is the "ability to apply knowledge and skills to achieve intended results." I prefer the Encarta dictionary definition: "The ability to do something well, measured against a standard, especially ability acquired through experience or training." For each task, the organization needs to establish a process to qualify the assigned employees, either by witnessing the employees work or through testing. Where job descriptions are used, the organization should provide a record of how and why the employee matches the job's requirements. The competence and training of temporary workers who perform the same tasks as employees in the plant should be included in the organization's training records.

Table 7.1 Focus of clauses for competence, awareness, and communication.

#	Clause	Focus	Objective evidence
7.2	Competence	Employee/temp ability to perform tasks within the QMS	Job descriptions; training records
7.3	Awareness	Employee understanding of the intent of the QMS and the quality objectives	Awareness meeting attendance; employee interviews
7.4	Communication	Changes in the QMS; employee contributions to improvement	Postings in the plant; employee interviews

> **Audit Questions**
>
> **Clause 7.2**
>
> *How does the organization determine the competence of personnel who perform work affecting conformity to product requirements?*
>
> *On what basis are new employees hired?*
>
> *How are employees moved to new assignments or cross-trained?*
>
> *How are new employees oriented and made aware of the organization's QMS?*
>
> *How does the organization make employees aware of the relevance and importance of their activities and how they contribute to the achievement of the quality objectives?*
>
> *How does the organization determine training needs?*
>
> *When procedures or work instructions change, how are impacted employees updated? How are these actions recorded?*
>
> **Clause 7.3**
>
> *How does the organization make employees aware of the intent and results of the QMS?*
>
> **Clause 7.4**
>
> *How does the organization communicate with the various levels and functions of the organization?*
>
> *How are changes affecting the QMS communicated to impacted employees?*
>
> *How does the organization receive, document, and respond to relevant communication from external interested parties?*
>
> *Is the quality policy available to the public? How?*

7.5 DOCUMENTED INFORMATION

> **7.5.1 General**
>
> The organization's quality management system shall include documented information required by this International Standard and documented information determined by the organization as being necessary for the effectiveness of the quality management system.
>
> **7.5.2 Creating and Updating**
>
> **When creating and updating documented information, the organization shall ensure appropriate:**
>
> - **Identification and description (e.g. a title, date, author or reference number);**
> - **Format (e.g. language, software version, graphics) and media (e.g. paper, electronic);**
> - **Review and approval for suitability and adequacy.**

> **7.5.3 Control of documented information**
>
> 7.5.3.1: Documented information required by the quality management system and by this International Standard shall be controlled to ensure:
>
> - It is available and suitable for use, where and when it is needed;
> - It is adequately protected (e.g. from loss of confidentiality, improper use or loss of integrity).
>
> 7.5.3.2: For the control of documented information, the organization shall address the following activities, as applicable:
>
> - Distribution, access, retrieval and use;
> - Storage and preservation, including preservation of legibility;
> - Control of changes (e.g. version control); retention and disposition.
>
> Documented information of external origin determined by the organization to be necessary for the planning and operation of the quality management system shall be identified as appropriate and be controlled.

A nomenclature change with ISO 9001:2015 is designating documented information as including both documents and records, which were defined independently in prior ISO 9001 revisions. This is consistent with ISO 14001:2015 and is intended to allow a variety of media to document the organization's plans. ISO 9000:2015 defines documented information as:

> Information required to be controlled and maintained by an organization and the medium on which it is contained. Documented information can be in any format and media, and from any source.

ISO 9001:2015 clause 7.5.2, Creating and updating, is more prescriptive than prior revisions of ISO 9001 as it defines how the organization should format their documented information. Procedures, work instructions, and forms need to include a title, date, author, or reference number; the format (e.g., software version, graphics); and whether the media is paper or electronic. The documented information needs to be reviewed and approved. With past revisions, the responsibilities for preparation of documents and approval were inconsistently interpreted by various organizations. The procedure describing the preparation of documented information should clearly define who will prepare documents (e.g., the process owner) and who will approve them (e.g., the quality manager, plant manager, or other authority). A best practice would be to have a minimum of two employees sign off on each document. If a third-party consultant assists the organization in preparing ISO 9001 documentation, a member of the organization's management needs to be part of the approval process.

The ISO 9001:2015 requirements for review and approval for suitability and adequacy are somewhat vague, as has been the case with prior ISO 9001 revisions. I suggest the organization establish a review process for documentation commensurate with the risks of deviation from employee instructions.

The intent of the review process should be to ensure that the quality documentation (e.g., work instructions, standard operating procedures) *matches current practices*. Operating personnel may improvise when performing a task to improve their efficiency or save steps, but this should not be done without management approval. The internal audit process may be a suitable method of monitoring documentation vs. practice, provided the audit notes include evidence that work instructions were validated. In other cases, work instructions should be reviewed by the appropriate authority at a defined frequency. I suggest that the organization establish a priority list, ranking the *risk level* of work instructions related to the potential for *quality upsets* (or prior history of error-prone activities). Examples might include the instructions for final release of sophisticated electronic devices or process conditions for chemical manufacturing. These instructions should be formally reviewed at least annually.

Clause 7.5.3, Control of documented information, differs from earlier ISO 9001 revisions in that documented information now covers what was previously referred to as quality records as well as procedures, instructions, and forms; it is also somewhat more prescriptive than prior revisions of ISO 9001, requiring the organization to establish a process to control the distribution, access, retrieval, use, storage, preservation (including preservation of legibility), changes (e.g., version control), retention, and disposition of all documented information. The majority of the requirements apply to quality records; however, the organization should also define its process for controlling the distribution, access, and version control of procedures, instructions, and forms.

Documents of external origin that the organization deems necessary for the planning and operation of the QMS need to be identified, as appropriate, and controlled. Examples of external documents include legal permits, licenses, laboratory analysis, supplier equipment manuals, and customer or industry requirements or specifications. A best practice for external document control would be to have a master list of all relevant external quality documents that specifies their location, how they are accessed, and how they are kept current, with the revision-level control process defined.

Quality records are a unique form of documented information. There is no requirement in ISO 9001:2015 indicating that organizations cannot use the term "quality record." ISO 9000:2015 defines documents and records as follows: "*Document*: information created in order for the organization to operate"; "*Record*: evidence of results achieved."

Quality records are an important part of the QMS. In addition to providing evidence of conformance to a specification or requirement, a quality record can be an organization's best defense against a customer product return or even a lawsuit. An extreme case where quality records were not properly maintained was the General Motors (GM) ignition switch failure starting in 2004, described here in a CNNMoney article:

> The essential problem: The cars' ignition switch, where the key is inserted and turned to start the car, could easily be bumped or moved out of the "Run" position into the "Off" or "Accessory" position. When that happens, power braking and steering, as well as airbags, can stop working....
>
> What most people at GM didn't know was that Delphi, the company that supplied the switch, had redesigned the part in 2006 to make it harder to turn.

The problem had been fixed. A GM engineer even signed off on the changes. Unfortunately, GM didn't change the part number of the switch. As a result, manufacturing records didn't indicate that the issue had been resolved. (Valdes-Dapena 2014)

The tragic ignition switch failure at GM is a prime example of a lack of both change control and quality record keeping. I have audited at companies where part number changes and part number drawing revision changes were not properly managed. When making changes, an organization needs to understand the difference between an F3 (form-fit-function) change and a drawing revision. A part drawing can be revised for clarity or ease in manufacturing, since the change will not impact the form, fit, or functionality of the part. Vista Industrial Products defines *fit*, *form*, and *function* as follows:

Fit: refers to the ability for the part to interconnect, mate with, join, or link to another part or an assembly. If a part requires "fit" it usually refers to having tight tolerances in order to match up to other parts or assembly.

Form: refers to dimensions, weight, size, and visual parameters of a part. This mainly represents the overall visual characteristics of the part.

Function: refers to the purpose of the part by how the part should perform and operate. (Vista Industrial Products 2012)

Because the ignition switch redesign provided improved *functionality*, making the switch harder to turn, the redesign should have resulted in a new part number. In my auditing experience at large companies with several levels of management, there is often bureaucracy involved in obtaining sign-off for new part numbers. The automotive sector in particular has a requirement for new part approval:

Production Part Approval Process (PPAP) defines requirements for production part approval, including production and bulk materials. The purpose of PPAP is to determine if all customer engineering design record and specification requirements are properly understood by the supplier and that the process has the potential to produce product consistently meeting these requirements during an actual production run at the quoted production rate. (AIAG 2006)

PPAP is a very powerful tool, particularly as it relates to change control and risks in product changes; however, the process takes time—and organizations take shortcuts. A drawing *revision change* requires fewer approval signatures and can be implemented quickly. Organizations using PPAP would be better off streamlining the approval process rather than bypassing it!

ISO 9001:2015 (like prior ISO 9001 revisions) does not require the creation and maintenance of a quality records list; however, it is a helpful tool for organizing various records. If a records list is not used, then each applicable quality record should be referenced in the related procedure or work instruction. An experienced auditor can use the organization's listing of records to drive an effective audit. Each record will create a trail, both forward and back, into how the organization is managing its quality commitments. How was the frequency of inspections or testing established: procedure? Why is the employee interviewed competent to do inspections: training record? Were the discrepancies that were noted in the internal audits resolved? What was learned from a customer complaint: follow-up actions?

The following are examples of quality records found in most organizations:

- Contract reviews
- Customer feedback
- Customer property
- Returned material
- Design reviews
- Engineering changes
- Approved supplier list
- Supplier evaluations
- Purchase orders
- Inspection reports
- Maintenance
- Calibration
- Work environment
- Employee training
- Corrective actions
- Improvement reports
- Audit reports
- Management review

An example of how a quality records list might be formatted is shown in Table 7.2.

Control of documented information requires the organization to control procedures and instructions that inform employees on how to complete their assigned tasks. In simple terms, any document or note that tells an employee how to do their job should be controlled. This doesn't mean a tip sheet or sketch posted on a machine to provide guidance on operating the machine must have a controlled document number assigned in the organization's QMS. The supervisor can "control" the tip sheet or sketch by initialing and dating it. It is good practice to place a limit on how long the tip sheet can stay in use—say, three months—before it is reapproved. A similar time limit should be placed on deviated changes to the controlled documents in the QMS (red-line notations).

I recently visited a former client, a precision welder of high-tech cylinders for the semiconductor industry. This company had posted work instructions at each work station providing detailed manufacturing and test information that was controlled in their documentation system and frequently accessed by the workers. I was surprised (and disappointed) to see each instruction now contained a "reference only" notation in large red letters. The company owner informed me

Table 7.2 Example of a records list.

Record title	Form #	Location	Type	Retention time	Disposition
Maintenance Records	F-101	Facility office	Copy	5 years	Archive
Returned Material Records	F-102	H drive	E-file	5 years	Archive

they had engaged a consultant to establish a lean manufacturing program. The consultant suggested that the company add the "reference only" notation so that when changes occurred, they would not have to worry about an ISO auditor challenging their document control. This misapplication of ISO document control is preached by many consultants and third-party auditors. *It is the antithesis of quality management.* Any instruction used by employees to complete a task cannot be "reference only"; it should reflect the most accurate and current information possible to avoid errors!

The "reference only" tactic has been around since the onset of ISO 9000. Organizations wanting to establish a solid QMS should avoid trying to beat the system and instead employ common sense when controlling documented information. Many organizations I've audited have been instructed by "experts" to add "This document is valid for three days after printing" (indicating that after three days the document is no longer valid, so employees should not use it) or a similar caveat to the footer of their documents. I advised these clients that this could only cause more difficulty and would not help them avoid a nonconformance. During the audits, I would sample several instructions that were in use, record their revision date, and verify the date against the master control list. If an instruction was out of date, then a gap in the organization's document system was evident. A "three days after printing" note only elevated the nonconformances. If an organization wants to use a caveat, a helpful message I've seen is: "It is the responsibility of the user to ensure the revision level is correct." The auditor still verifies the currency of the instruction; however, now the onus is on the employee using the instruction to take ownership of the accuracy of instructions for his or her work.

I witnessed a rather comical overuse of "reference only" stamps while auditing a company that supplied machined components to the automotive sector. In touring the plant, I observed a large poster: "The Decimal–Fraction Conversion Chart." It had the "reference only" notation.

Audit Questions

Clause 7.5

Where are the following documented?

- The quality policy, objectives, and programs
- Description of the scope, boundaries, and context of the QMS

How does the organization describe the main elements of the QMS and their relationship with ISO 9001:2015?

What documented information of the QMS is necessary for the organization to maintain the effectiveness of the QMS?

How does the organization provide linkage or reference to lower-level documentation?

How are external documents maintained?
Examples: Customer specifications, product or material drawings, regulatory documents, quality standards, supplier manuals

How does the organization define the process for approving documents for adequacy prior to issue?

How does the organization define the process for preparing documents to include:
- The identification and description (e.g., a title, date, author, or reference number)?
- The format (e.g., language, software version, graphics) and media (e.g., paper, electronic)?

How does the organization control the processes for:
- Ensuring that relevant versions of applicable documents are available at points of use?
- Preventing the unintended use of obsolete documents and ensuring that the documents remain legible and readily identifiable?

How does the organization control the process for reviewing and updating procedures and work instructions to ensure they are being used by employees as documented?

How does the organization control the process for changing documents and providing revision control and record of change?

How does the organization protect documented information retained as evidence of conformity from unintended alteration?

How does the organization identify, store, and protect records required to demonstrate conformity to its QMS?
- Is the retention time for records defined?
- What is the process used to dispose of records?

Where are the quality records identified?
Examples: Records list, procedure, work instruction

How are the quality records accessed?

8
Clause 8: Operation

#	ISO 9001:2015	#	ISO 9001:2008
8	Operation	7	Product realization
8.1	Operational planning and control	7.1	Planning of product realization
8.2	Requirements for products and services	7.2.1	Determination of requirements related to the product
8.2.1	Customer communication	7.2.3	Customer communication
8.2.2	Determining the requirements related to products and services	7.2.2	Review of requirements related to the product
8.2.3	Review of requirements related to products and services	7.2.2	Review of requirements related to the product
8.2.4	Changes to requirements for products and services	7.2.2	Review of requirements related to the product
8.3	Design and development of products and services	7.3	Design and development
8.3.1	General	7.3.1	Design and development planning
8.3.2	Design and development planning	7.3.1	Design and development planning
8.3.3	Design and development inputs	7.3.2	Design and development inputs
8.3.4	Design and development controls	7.3.4 7.3.5 7.3.6	Design and development review Design and development verification Design and development validation
8.3.5	Design and development outputs	7.3.3	Design and development outputs
8.3.6	Design and development changes	7.3.7	Control of design and development changes
8.4	Control of externally provided processes, products and services	7.4.1	Purchasing process
8.4.1	General	7.4.1	Purchasing process
8.4.2	Type and extent of control	7.4.1 7.4.3 4.1	Purchasing process Verification of purchased product General requirements (outsourcing)
8.4.3	Information for external providers	7.4.2	Purchasing information
8.5	Production and service provision	7.5	Production and service provision
8.5.1	Control of production and service provision	7.5.1 7.5.2	Control of production and service provision Validation of processes for production and service provision
8.5.2	Identification and traceability	7.5.3	Identification and traceability

#	ISO 9001:2015	#	ISO 9001:2008
8.5.3	Property belonging to customers or external providers	7.5.4	Customer property
8.5.4	Preservation	7.5.5	Preservation of product
8.5.5	Post-delivery activities	7.5.1	Control of production and service provision
8.5.6	Control of changes	7.2.2	Review of requirements related to the product
8.6	Release of products and services	8.2.4	Monitoring and measurement of product
8.7	Control of nonconforming outputs	8.3	Control of nonconforming product

Clause 8 includes subclauses from ISO 9001:2008 clause 7, Product realization, along with clause 8.2.4, Monitoring and measurement of product, and clause 8.3, Control of nonconforming product. Additionally, 4.1, General requirements (outsourcing), is now included in clause 8 of ISO 9001:2015. ISO 9001:2015 does not add any new requirements for operational control. "Control of externally provided processes, products and services" is new terminology introduced to define the requirements for purchasing and outsourced processes. This change attempts to ensure that organizations involved in *services* have equal footing with organizations that make *products*. The use of the term "externally provided processes" helps distinguish purchased materials from outsourced activities. The process chart in Figure 8.1 provides a road map for the subclauses of clause 8. Note: In Chapter 8, *service* will be regarded as the product of the organization.

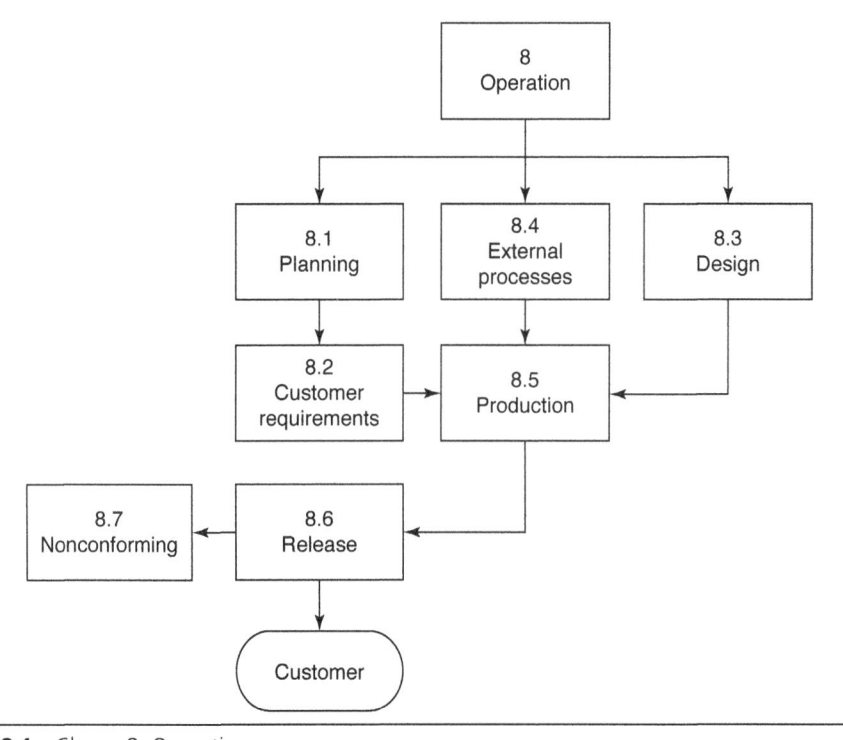

Figure 8.1 Clause 8: Operation.

8.1 OPERATIONAL PLANNING AND CONTROL

> The organization shall implement and control the processes needed to meet the requirements for the provision of products and services. The organization's planning shall include:
>
> - Determination of the requirements for the products and services;
> - Establishing criteria for the processes and for the acceptance of products and services;
> - Actions to address risks and opportunities.
>
> The organization shall:
>
> - Determine the resources needed to achieve conformity to the product and service requirements;
> - Implement control of the processes in accordance with the criteria;
> - Determine and keep documented information (records) to the extent necessary to have confidence that the processes have been carried out as planned and to demonstrate the products and services conform to their requirements.
>
> The output of this planning shall be suitable for the organization's operations.
> 	The organization shall control planned changes and review the consequences of unintended changes, taking action to mitigate any adverse effects, as necessary.
> 	The organization shall ensure that outsourced processes are controlled.

Clause 8.1 is the "executive summary" for operational planning and control. A third-party auditor will use this clause to get "calibrated" with the organization's operations: the quality specifications and requirements for the product or service; the measurement, inspection, and test activities; and the criteria for product acceptance. Subsequent clauses define the precise requirements related to the organization's manufacturing or service processes.

8.2 REQUIREMENTS FOR PRODUCTS AND SERVICES

> ### 8.2.1 Customer communication
>
> Communications with customers shall include:
>
> - Providing information relating to products and services;
> - Handling inquiries, contracts or orders, including changes;
> - Obtaining customer feedback relating to products and services, including customer complaints;
> - Handling or controlling customer property;
> - Establishing specific requirements for **contingency actions**, when relevant.
>
> ### 8.2.2 Determining the requirements related to products and services
>
> When determining the requirements for the products and services to be offered to customers, the organization shall ensure that the requirements for the products and services are defined, including any applicable statutory and regulatory requirements and those considered necessary by the organization.
> 	The organization shall ensure that it can meet the claims for the products and services it offers.

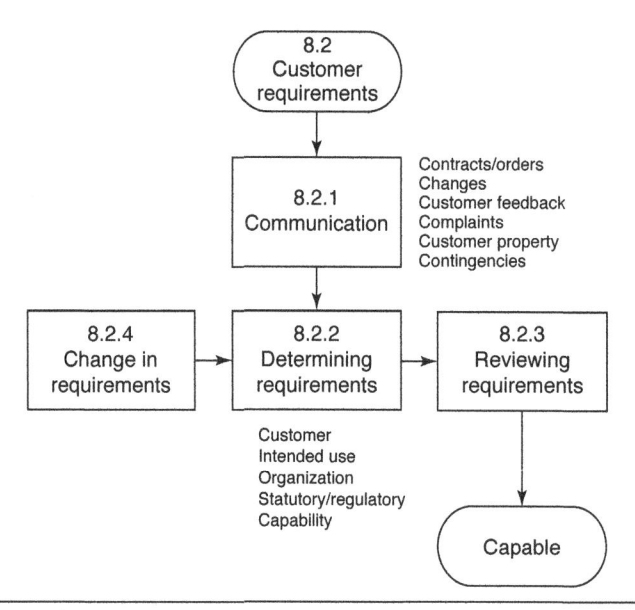

Figure 8.2 Understanding customer requirements and determining capability.

Clause 8.2.1 requires that the organization establish a process to communicate with its customers in relation to:

- Product information
- Sales inquiries
- Contracts or order handling
- Changes to orders
- Customer complaints
- Customer feedback

Under clause 8.2.2, the organization needs to determine how customer requirements are established. What format is used by the organization to record customer requirements? How does the organization ensure that changes to product requirements are defined and resolved? How does the organization establish specific requirements for contingency actions, when relevant to the customer's requirements? Most importantly, does the organization have the capability to meet customer requirements? In past ISO 9001 revisions, the capability to fulfill a customer requirement was referred to as contract review, which is now defined in clause 8.2.3.

8.2.3 Review of requirements related to products and services

8.2.3.1: The organization shall ensure that it has the ability to meet the requirements for products and services to be offered to customers.

The organization shall conduct a review before committing to supply products and services to a customer to include:

- Requirements specified by the customer, including the requirements for delivery and post-delivery activities;

> - Requirements not stated by the customer, but necessary for the specified or intended use, when known;
> - Requirements specified by the organization;
> - Statutory and regulatory requirements applicable to the products and services;
> - Contract or order requirements differing from those previously expressed.
>
> The organization shall ensure that contract or order requirements differing from those previously defined are resolved. The customer's requirements shall be confirmed by the organization before acceptance when the customer does not provide a documented statement of their requirements.
>
> 8.2.3.2: The organization shall retain documented information as applicable on the results of the review and on any new requirements for the products and services.
>
> **8.2.4 Changes to requirements for products and services**
>
> The organization shall ensure that relevant documented information is amended, and that relevant persons are made aware of the changed requirements, when the requirements for products and services are changed.

The organization needs to ensure it has the capability to produce the product or provide the service as defined by the customer—i.e., does it have the equipment, processes, and resources required to meet the customer's product delivery dates or service commitment?

Appropriate requirements from external agencies such as regulations on product safety and chemicals or materials used in the product need to be followed. The National Electrical Manufacturers Association (NEMA), the association of electrical equipment and medical imaging manufacturers, provides requirements for the standardization of electrical equipment. The Food and Drug Administration (FDA), which is responsible for protecting and promoting public health in the United States, regulates food safety in both manufacturing processes and products. Other external agencies, such as the American National Standards Institute (ANSI) and the American Society for Testing Materials (ASTM), may have applications for the organization related to testing.

A record of the organization's analysis and review of the customer's requirements needs to be maintained. When changes occur, either by customer request or due to internal issues, the organization must document the changes with approvals or acknowledgment as appropriate.

A metric or monitoring plan should be established for each customer (or core) process to measure the effectiveness of the process and to establish a baseline for improvement of the organization's planning/sales, design, external (purchasing), and production processes. Table 8.1 lists some examples of metrics that can be used to track performance in planning or sales processes.

Once a metric is established, a goal should be set. In many privately held organizations, sales revenue information is well guarded. In those cases, the "sales performance against sales plan as a percent" metric can be useful. For many organizations, "bid success rate" (or "hit rate") can measure how well the sales department is performing. A low trend in bid success rate can be alarming for obvious reasons. I've also seen cases where a company producing commodity products

Table 8.1 Examples of metrics for sales process.

Core process	Possible metrics
Sales	$ revenue; $ revenue per employee; sales performance against sales plan as %; bid success rate
Order entry	Order entry errors
Contract review	On-time delivery; actual cost vs. estimate

becomes concerned when the bid success rate trends high, since this could mean the company is setting its prices too low compared to the competition.

Audit Questions

Clause 8.1

When planning to produce a product or provide a service, how does the organization determine:

- *The quality specifications and requirements for the product or service?*
- *The need to establish processes—documents and resources specific to the product or service?*
- *The measurement, inspection, and test activities specific to the product or service?*
- *The criteria for product acceptance?*

What records are needed to provide evidence that the product or service meets customer requirements?

Clause 8.2.1

How does the organization communicate with its customers in relation to:

- *Product information?*
- *Inquiries?*
- *Contracts or orders, including changes to orders?*

How does the organization determine customer requirements?

What format is used by the organization to record customer requirements?

How does the organization ensure that changes to product requirements are defined and resolved?

How does the organization establish specific requirements for contingency actions, when relevant to the customer's requirements?

What is the process for handling customer feedback and customer complaints?

Clause 8.2.2

How does the organization ensure that product requirements are defined?

How are the product requirements recorded in the organization's QMS?

> *What statutory and regulatory requirements are applicable to the organization's products or services?*
>
> *How does the organization ensure the applicable regulatory requirements are maintained?*
>
> Examples: Product safety laws, regulations on chemicals or materials used in the product, electrical standards, FDA regulations
>
> *How does the organization ensure it has the capability to produce the product or provide the service as defined by the customer?*
>
> Examples: Process/resource capability, ability to meet customer product delivery time or service commitment
>
> *What method is used to monitor or, where applicable, measure the sales process? (See also clause 9.1.)*

8.3 DESIGN AND DEVELOPMENT OF PRODUCTS AND SERVICES

> **8.3.1 General**
>
> The organization shall establish, implement and maintain a design and development process that is appropriate to ensure the subsequent provision of products and services.
>
> **8.3.2 Design and development planning**
>
> In determining the stages and controls for design and development, the organization shall consider:
>
> - The nature, duration and complexity of the design and development activities;
> - The required process stages, including applicable reviews;
> - Design and development verification and validation activities;
> - Responsibilities and authorities;
> - Internal and external resource needs;
> - Control interfaces between persons involved;
> - The need for customer and user involvement;
> - Requirements for subsequent provision of products and services;
> - The level of control expected by customers and other relevant interested parties;
> - The documented information needed to demonstrate requirements have been met.
>
> **8.3.3 Design and development inputs**
>
> The organization shall determine the requirements essential for the specific types of products and services to be designed and developed.
>   The organization shall consider: functional and performance requirements; information derived from previous similar design and development activities; statutory and regulatory requirements; standards or codes of practice; potential consequences of failure.

> Inputs shall be adequate for design and development purposes, complete and unambiguous. Conflicting design and development inputs shall be resolved.
>
> **8.3.4 Design and development controls**
>
> The organization shall apply controls to ensure: the results to be achieved are defined; reviews are conducted to evaluate the ability of the results to meet requirements; verification activities are conducted; validation activities are conducted; necessary actions are taken on problems determined during the reviews, or verification and validation activities; documented information of these activities is retained.
>
> **8.3.5 Design and development outputs**
>
> The organization shall ensure that design and development outputs: meet the input requirements; are adequate for the subsequent processes; include or reference monitoring and measuring requirements, acceptance criteria, characteristics of the products and services that are essential for their intended purpose and their safe and proper provision.
>
> **8.3.6 Design and development changes**
>
> The organization shall identify, review and control changes made during, or subsequent to, the design and development of products and services, to the extent necessary to ensure that there is no adverse impact on conformity to requirements. The organization shall retain documented information on: design and development changes; the results of reviews; the authorization of the changes; the actions taken to prevent adverse impacts.

Clause 8.3 has the same requirements as ISO 9001:2008 clause 7.3, Design and development; however, the 2015 revision more clearly recognizes that there can be major differences in *complexity* among design and development activities within the organization. The general requirements for clause 8.3 cover design processes for projects with a cycle time of a few years and also for projects completed in days or weeks (enhancements/modifications or minor reconfiguration of mature designs). Organizations with both complex, lengthy projects and quick-turnaround modifications should develop their design process controls accordingly.

Not explicitly stated in the requirements is the need to have a *time-bound plan*. This has been a deficiency in prior revisions of ISO 9001 as well. When auditing an organization with several designers and several projects running simultaneously, I am often disappointed to observe the lack of an integrated plan to assist in scheduling resources. While the required stages of the project are defined, the planned completion dates or milestones are not established (or estimated). Many organizations use a Gantt chart, or something similar, to establish estimated completion dates for each design stage—often working backward from the customer's required completion date. When the timelines of all projects are integrated, resources can be better allocated.

In simple terms, the basic requirement for a design project includes:

- Statement of work—what is "new"?
- Time-bound plan
- Input requirements—specifications
- Outputs—expectations

- Design reviews as appropriate
- Verification/validation plan

An overview of the design process is given in Figure 8.3.

Dr. Robert G. Cooper, one of the founders of Stage-Gate International, introduced a product development process called the Stage-Gate innovation process over 20 years ago. Many organizations have used this process or a variation of it to satisfy the requirements of the ISO 9001 design clause. An internet search yields many software product offerings related to Stage-Gate (sometimes referred to as *phase-gate*). A properly designed and implemented Stage-Gate process would satisfy the requirements of ISO 9001:2015 clause 8.3 and add two enhancements while integrating ISO 9001 with the organization's business model. Stage 1 includes a *screening* of ideas for new developments to analyze the cost benefits of the project along with potential challenges and competitive factors. The last stage (often Stage 8) includes a *post-launch review* to measure the project's results and return on investment, as well as lessons learned to apply to future projects. I recommend the use of some form of the Stage-Gate process for organizations of any size or level of complexity. See Appendix C for a summary of Stage-Gate.

A model I developed of a generic ISO 9001 Stage-Gate process is shown in Figure 8.4.

In the design Stage-Gate process, a customer-driven project is a project requested by a customer. A design project initiated by the management of the organization to serve many customers, or a general consumer-based project, may

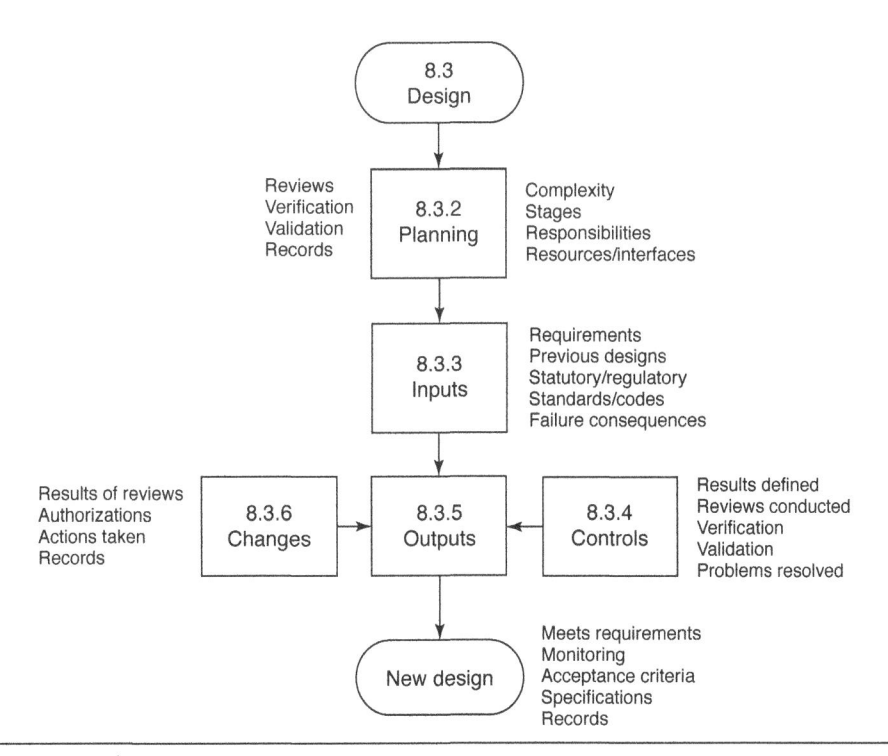

Figure 8.3 Design process.

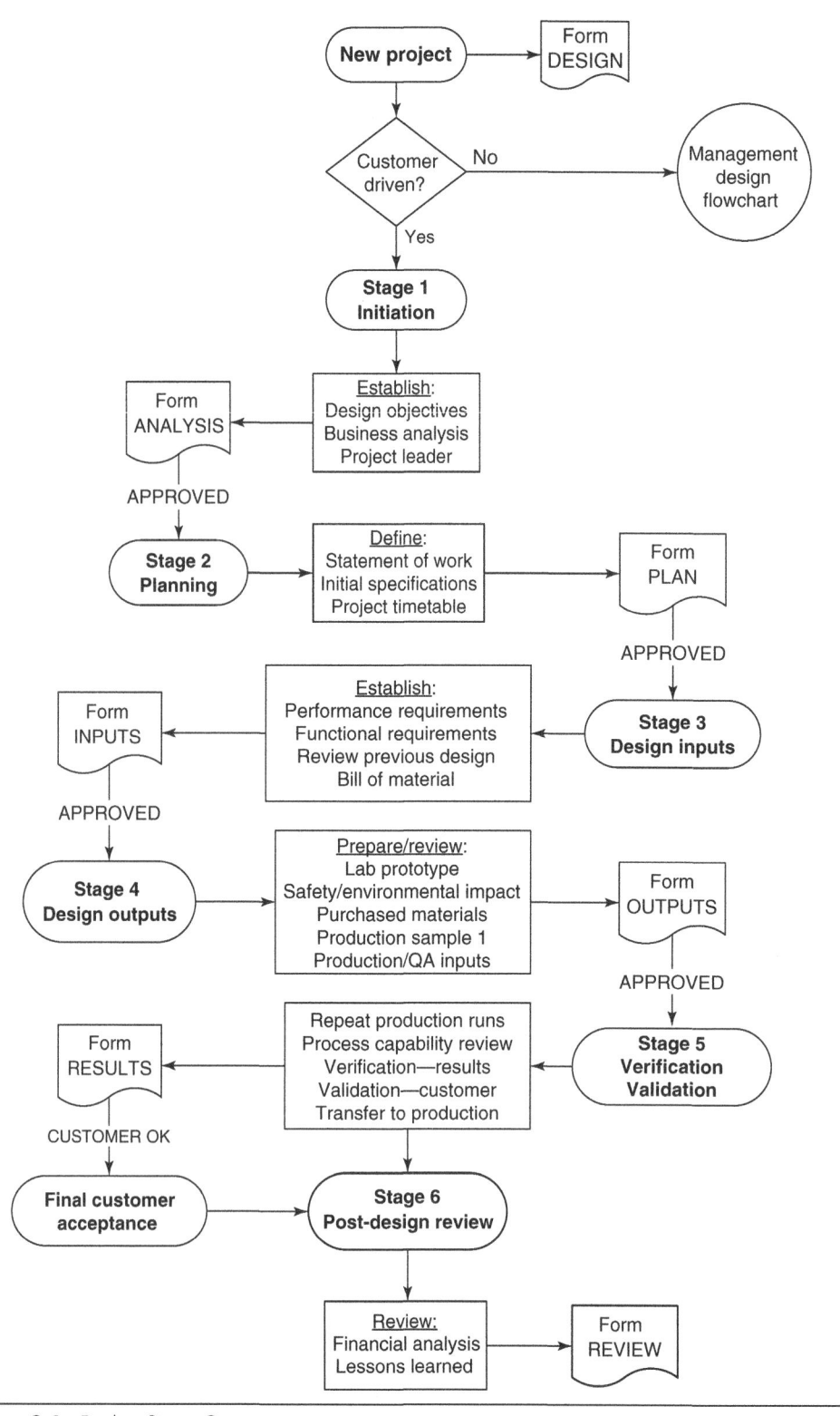

Figure 8.4 Design Stage-Gate process.

Table 8.2 Contents of forms in design Stage-Gate process.

Stage	Form	Contents
Start	DESIGN	Date; customer; contact; unit manager; sales representative; product description; pricing target; other information
1	ANALYSIS	Design objectives; business analysis; project leader
2	PLAN	Statement of work; initial specifications; project timetable
3	INPUT	Performance/functional requirements; regulatory impact; previous design review; bill of material
4	OUTPUT	Lab prototype; safety/environmental impact; purchased materials; production sample 1; production/QA input
5	RESULTS	Repeat production runs; process capability review; verification—customer results; validation at customer; transfer to production
6	REVIEW	Financial analysis; lessons learned

require more stages, similar to the Stage-Gate International process. The customer-driven model can be used for enhancements/modifications or minor reconfiguration of mature designs or for more complex designs with long cycle times. In the case of minor reconfiguration projects with short cycle times, the forms can be designed to allow for the consolidation of several steps, requiring less paperwork and fewer approvals. Table 8.2 lists some of the related design records from the referenced forms.

A metric or monitoring plan should be established for the design process to measure the effectiveness of the process and to establish a baseline for improvement. A design-oriented organization jeopardizes its ability to maintain or increase sales revenue if it does not offer new products to replace products obsoleted by its customers or market sector. Many organizations I've audited establish a goal for the design group to create incremental annual sales generated by new designs at 15%–20% of current sales to offset obsoleted or poor-selling products. Examples of metrics used to track performance in the design process include:

- Sales revenue for new design projects as a percentage of annual sales
- Percentage of design projects that create sales revenue
- Cycle time to complete projects
- Percentage of design projects completed on time and on budget

> **Audit Questions**
>
> **Clause 8.3**
>
> *How does the organization determine the design and development stages of a new design, and how does it establish a process to review the progress of the design?*
>
> *Is there a project plan with timelines defined?*
>
> *How does the organization determine:*
> - Verification and validation processes?
> - Responsibilities and authorities?

> *In a design project, how does the organization determine:*
> - Functional and performance requirements?
> - Applicable statutory and regulatory requirements?
> - Information derived from previous similar designs, if applicable?
> - Other requirements essential for design and development?
>
> *How do the design reviews evaluate the ability of the results (or progress) of the design to meet requirements and record problems identified during the design process with actions proposed to resolve them?*
>
> *How does the organization verify the design?*
> (Verification = meets requirements of the design input specifications.)
>
> *How does the organization validate the design?*
> (Validation = satisfies the customer's intended use of the design or product. In some cases, the customer may take responsibility for the validation process.)
>
> *How does the organization manage changes during the design steps?*
>
> *What method is used to monitor or, where applicable, measure the design process? (See also clause 9.1.)*

8.4 CONTROL OF EXTERNALLY PROVIDED PROCESSES, PRODUCTS AND SERVICES

> ### 8.4.1 General
>
> The organization shall ensure that externally provided processes, products and services conform to requirements.
>   The organization shall determine the controls to be applied to externally provided processes, products and services when:
>
> - Products and services from external providers are incorporated into the organization's own products and services;
> - Products and services are provided directly to the customers by external providers on behalf of the organization;
> - A process, or part of a process, is provided by an external provider.
>
> The organization shall determine and apply criteria for the evaluation, selection, monitoring of performance and reevaluation of external providers or products and services in accordance with requirements.
>
> ### 8.4.2 Type and extent of control
>
> The organization shall ensure that externally provided processes, products and services do not adversely affect the organization's ability to consistently deliver conforming products and services to its customers.
>   The organization shall ensure that externally provided processes remain within the control of its quality management system and define both the controls that it intends to apply to an external provider and those it intends to apply to the resulting output.

> The organization shall take into consideration the potential impact of the externally provided processes, products and services on the organization's ability to consistently meet customer and applicable statutory and regulatory requirements and the effectiveness of the controls applied by the external provider.
>
> The organization shall determine the verification, or other activities, necessary to ensure that the externally provided processes, products and services meet requirements.
>
> **8.4.3 Information for external providers**
>
> The organization shall ensure the adequacy of requirements prior to their communication to the external provider. The organization shall communicate to external providers its requirements for:
>
> - The processes, products and services to be provided;
> - The approval of products and services, methods, processes and equipment;
> - The release of products and services;
> - Competence, including any required qualification of persons;
> - The external providers' interactions with the organization;
> - The control and monitoring of the external providers' performance to be applied by the organization;
> - The verification or validation activities that the organization, or its customer, intends to perform at the external providers' premises.

Externally provided processes were referred to as purchasing and outsourcing in previous versions of ISO 9001. ISO 9001:2015 does not add any new purchasing process requirements. Combining outsourcing and purchasing in the same clause may clarify the differences between the two external processes. A process chart for external processes is depicted in Figure 8.5.

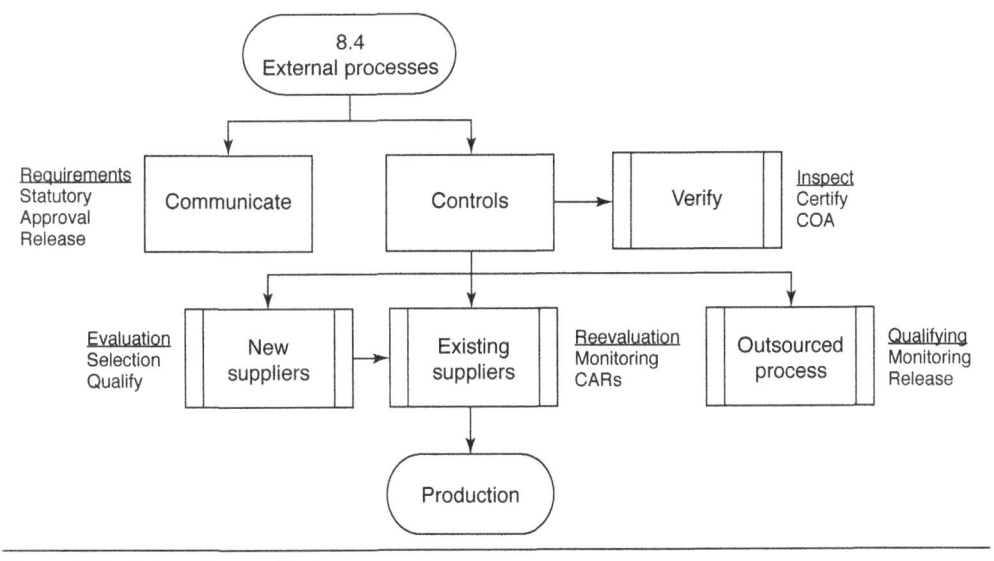

Figure 8.5 Externally provided processes.

ISO 9001:2015 does not define outsourced processes. ISO 9001:2008 clause 4.1, General requirements, provided the following definition of an outsourced process:

> A process that the organization needs for its quality management system, and which the organization chooses to have performed by an external party.

When an organization purchases materials, products, or services, it is *choosing* to have an external party perform a process. Outsourcing, in the context of ISO 9001, has been a source of inconsistent interpretation for several years. ISO 9001:2015 does not provide a clear definition. My preferred definition of outsourcing is:

> Materials, products, or services provided for the organization's customers by external providers and shipped directly from the external provider's site to the organization's customers.

The logic behind this definition centers on *risk* and *control*.

For example, say an organization engages an external source (a supplier) to chrome-plate parts. If the supplier returns the chrome-plated parts to the organization, that is *purchasing*. If the supplier delivers the chrome-plated parts directly to the organization's customer, that is *outsourcing*.

In the purchasing scenario, the organization can inspect the parts before releasing them to the customer. In the outsourcing scenario, the organization has to rely on the chrome-plating supplier to properly inspect, package, and ship the finished product to the organization's customer. This adds the risk that the supplier will not perform the tasks properly. When outsourcing is used in this context, the organization needs to *establish controls* to monitor the supplier's quality. Controls for outsourced sources include a wide range of activities depending on the quality risk of the outsourced activity. At the high end of risk, the outsourced provider is required to transmit inspection or functionality results to the organization requesting the work, before shipping the product to the organization's customer. Other high-risk-level outsourced processes are managed by having a representative of the organization release the product at the provider's plant. Lower-level controls include certifying the provider through performance history and/or quality audits at the provider's plant.

This outsourcing scenario is related to ISO 9001 clause 8, Operation. There are other outsourced processes related to human resources, information technology (IT), and accounting that require controls appropriate to the activities and risk. When design activities are outsourced, the potential impact on customer requirements is normally controlled by the hiring organization's approval of the outsourced designer's work.

The process and criteria established to *evaluate and select new suppliers* need to be commensurate with the impact the supplier has on the organization's quality performance. For an original equipment manufacturer (OEM), where the performance of suppliers is critical, a detailed new supplier review process may be in order. A machine shop that purchases standard materials from a distributor may have a less detailed process. In all cases, there should be a documented plan that matches the organization's business model. While a potential new supplier holding an ISO 9001 third-party certificate should be congratulated, they still need to be evaluated using defined criteria!

The process and criteria used by the organization to *reevaluate approved suppliers* needs to be determined, also according to the supplier's criticality. The OEM might track its supplier's performance in quality, delivery, and service; the machine shop might use the corrective action process to communicate the supplier's performance.

Good quality and business management requires the organization to maintain a process for *authorizing purchase orders* to external providers with a clear statement of what is to be provided. The verification or validation activities that the organization performs at the supplier's premises (if applicable) should be clearly defined.

The organization needs to determine which purchased materials *require inspection* to ensure purchased product meets specified purchase requirements. If no inspection is required, how did the supplier become certified? Many organizations that purchase chemicals or paper or plastic substrates require that either COAs or certificates of conformance (COCs) be delivered with the received material. A process should be established for reviewing and approving the certificates for conformance to requirements.

A *metric or monitoring plan* should be established for the purchasing process to measure the effectiveness of the process and to establish a baseline for improvement. A common metric is a representation of the delivery and quality performance of suppliers. In large consumer-oriented companies or contract manufacturers, a common metric is purchased price variance (PPV). PPV connects the purchasing performance to the organization's business performance by establishing spending reductions in material costs to improve profits.

Audit Questions

Clause 8.4

What process and criteria are used by the organization to evaluate new suppliers?

What process and criteria are used by the organization to reevaluate approved suppliers?

How does the organization control and monitor the performance of suppliers?

How does the organization maintain the listing of approved suppliers?

How does the organization manage the release of purchase orders to suppliers?

How does the organization determine which purchased materials require inspection to ensure purchased product meets specified purchase requirements?

Describe the verification or validation activities that the organization performs at the supplier's premises (if applicable).

How does the organization control outsourced processes? Where are the controls defined?

What method is used to monitor or, where applicable, measure the purchasing process? (See also clause 9.1.)

8.5 PRODUCTION AND SERVICE PROVISION

8.5.1 Control of production and service provision

The organization shall implement production and service provision under controlled conditions.
   Controlled conditions shall include, as applicable:

- The availability of documented information that defines the characteristics of the products to be produced, the services to be provided, or the activities to be performed and the results to be achieved;
- The availability and use of suitable monitoring and measuring resources;
- The implementation of monitoring and measurement activities at appropriate stages to verify that criteria for control of processes or outputs, and acceptance criteria for products and services, have been met;
- The use of suitable infrastructure and environment for the operation of processes;
- The appointment of competent persons, including any required qualification;
- The validation, and periodic revalidation, of the ability to achieve planned results of the processes for production and service provision, where the resulting output cannot be verified by subsequent monitoring or measurement;
- The implementation of actions to prevent human error;
- The implementation of release, delivery and post-delivery activities.

8.5.2 Identification and traceability

The organization shall use suitable means to identify outputs when it is necessary to ensure the conformity of products and services. The organization shall identify the status of outputs with respect to monitoring and measurement requirements throughout production and service provision.
   The organization shall control the unique identification of the outputs when traceability is a requirement, and shall retain the documented information necessary to enable traceability.

8.5.3 Property belonging to customers or external providers

The organization shall exercise care with property belonging to customers or external providers while it is under the organization's control or being used by the organization.
   The organization shall identify, verify, protect and safeguard customers' or external providers' property provided for use or incorporation into the products and services.
   When the property of a customer or external provider is lost, damaged or otherwise found to be unsuitable for use, the organization shall report this to the customer or external provider.

8.5.4 Preservation

The organization shall preserve the outputs during production and service provision, to the extent necessary to ensure conformity to requirements. NOTE: Preservation can include identification, handling, contamination control, packaging, storage, transmission or transportation and protection.

8.5.5 Post-delivery activities

The organization shall meet requirements for post-delivery activities associated with the products and services, considering statutory and regulatory requirements; the potential undesired consequences associated with its products and services; the nature, use and intended lifetime of its products and services; and customer requirements and customer feedback.

Post-delivery activities can include actions under warranty provisions, contractual obligations such as maintenance services, and supplementary services such as recycling or final disposal.

8.5.6 Control of changes

The organization shall review and control changes for production or service provision, to the extent necessary to ensure continuing conformity with requirements.

The organization shall retain documented information describing the results of the review of changes, the persons authorizing the change and any necessary actions arising from the review.

8.6 RELEASE OF PRODUCTS AND SERVICES

The organization shall implement planned arrangements, at appropriate stages, to verify that the product and service requirements have been met.

The release of products and services to the customer shall not proceed until the planned arrangements have been satisfactorily completed, unless otherwise approved by a relevant authority and, as applicable, by the customer.

The organization shall include documented information on the release of products and services to include evidence of conformity with the acceptance criteria and traceability to the persons authorizing the release.

8.7 CONTROL OF NONCONFORMING OUTPUTS

8.7.1: The organization shall ensure that outputs that do not conform to their requirements are identified and controlled to prevent their unintended use or delivery.

The organization shall take appropriate action based on the nature of the nonconformity and its effect on the conformity of products and services. This shall also apply to nonconforming products and services detected after delivery of products, during or after the provision of services.

The organization shall deal with nonconforming outputs in one or more of the following ways: correction, segregation, containment, return or suspension of provision of products and services.

The organization shall inform the customer to obtain authorization for acceptance under concession. Conformity to the requirements shall be verified when nonconforming outputs are corrected.

8.7.2: The organization shall retain documented information that describes the nonconformity; the actions taken; and any concessions obtained. The organization shall identify the authority deciding the action in respect of the nonconformity.

ISO 9001:2015 does not present any new requirements for production or service. Clauses 8.5, 8.6, and 8.7 consolidate the ISO 9001:2008 requirements of clause 7.5, Production and service provision; clause 8.2.4, Monitoring and measurement of product; and clause 8.3, Control of nonconforming product. A process chart for clauses 8.5–8.7 is shown in Figure 8.6. (Guidelines for service type organizations are included at the end of Chapter 8).

ISO 9001:2015 removed a main clause from ISO 9001:2008—clause 7.5.2, Validation of processes—and moved the requirement into clause 8.5.1, Control of production and service provision:

ISO 9001:2008 clause 7.5.2, Validation of processes for production and service provision

The organization shall validate any processes for production and service provision where the resulting output cannot be verified by subsequent monitoring or measurement and, as a consequence, deficiencies become apparent only after the product is in use or the service has been delivered.

ISO 9001:2015 clause 8.5.1, Control of production and service provision

Controlled conditions shall include the validation, and periodic revalidation, of the ability to achieve planned results of the processes for production and service provision, where the resulting output cannot be verified by subsequent monitoring or measurement and the implementation of release, delivery and post-delivery activities.

This is unfortunate, in my opinion, as validation of processes can be an important facet of an organization's quality performance and is often overlooked by both auditors and organizations. Under ISO 9001:2008, if an organization did not have a reason to validate processes, clause 7.5.2 was excluded with justification as to why validation was not required. If an organization can measure its products, either by dimensional, functional, or visual standards, the validation requirements do not

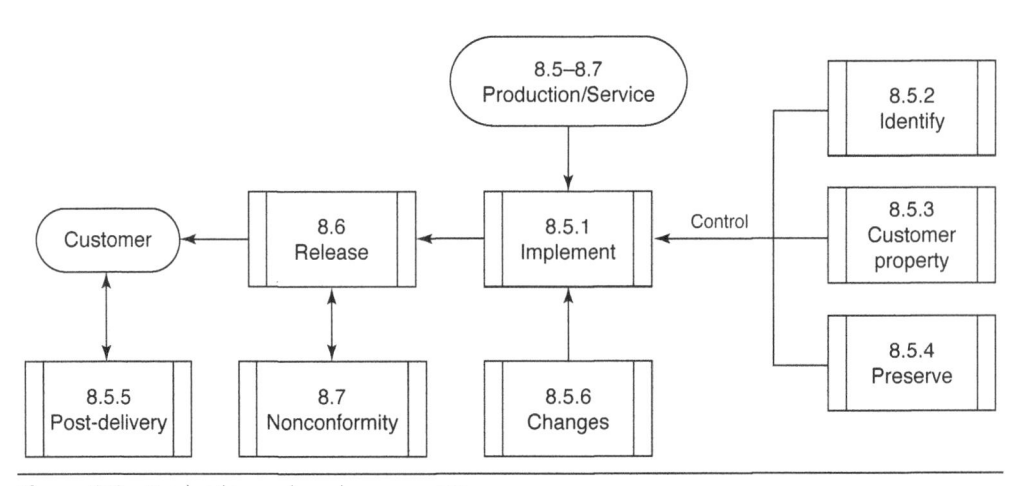

Figure 8.6 Production and service processes.

apply. Examples where validation is required to ensure a product does not have deficiencies when delivered to the customer include:

- Soldering (where integrity of joints cannot be verified by measurement)
- Welding
- Machine assembly
- Cleaning
- Lamination
- Coating or painting
- Heat treating or plating

In these cases, the manufacturer cannot ensure that the product meets requirements without destroying the product (or validating the employees or equipment); thus, a *process validation* is needed. In the case of soldering, welding, or machine assembly, training and certifying the employees doing the work is a way to validate that the process is under control. For cleaning or lamination, a representative sample may have to be destroyed at some frequency to validate that the process has been cleaning the product or that the equipment is producing adequate lamination. In coating, painting, heat treating, or plating, a sample or coupon can be exposed to the process and then measured to validate that the entire lot has the required thickness or other characteristics.

The other clauses in this group have not changed from the 2008 revision. Following are some suggestions on how an organization can manage its production or service provisions, quality inspections, preservation of materials, nonconforming outputs, and post-delivery activities:

- *Control of production and service provision:* The organization needs to provide information and characteristics required to produce the product or service as well as the methods or instructions used to ensure the product or service is produced as planned. Depending on the type of manufacturing, the information can be in the form of a "traveler," which is created from the work order and includes instructions, material list, drawings, inspection plans, process steps, and process conditions. If the required information is in the traveler, there may not be a need for a work instruction.

- The quality inspections need to be planned, from approval of the raw material to in-process inspections to inspections releasing material to the next process. The organization needs to *identify the product status* with respect to inspection or monitoring requirements throughout manufacturing. Changes to the information and characteristics required to produce the product or service need to be managed, including authorities and deviation processes. The authorization process to approve products or services for release to customers should be defined and controlled.

- The organization needs to ensure that materials and components are *preserved* during processing and delivery to the organization's customers and during processing of materials to protect the product. Adhesives, sealants, coatings, paints, desiccants, and solder-paste/flux have shelf-life concerns and need to be monitored.

- *Control of nonconforming outputs:* The organization needs to ensure that product that does not conform to requirements is properly identified and controlled to prevent its unintended use or delivery. How does the organization take action to eliminate the detected nonconformity? What actions are taken by the organization when the nonconforming product is detected after delivery or use has started? How does the organization verify that nonconforming product that has been corrected conforms to the intended requirements? How does the organization analyze nonconforming product occurrences to prevent reoccurrence?

- Any *post-delivery activities* applicable to the organization need to be planned and controlled. Examples include warranty provisions, contractual obligations (e.g., maintenance services), and supplementary services (e.g., recycling or final disposal).

A *metric or monitoring plan* should be established for the production process to measure the effectiveness of the process and to establish a baseline for improvement. Common metrics are on-time delivery (OTD), percentage defective at customers, material yield, productivity (employee labor hours), and internal waste.

Audit Questions

Clause 8.5.1

How does the organization provide the information and characteristics required to produce the product or service?

What methods or instructions are used to ensure the product is produced as planned?

How are changes to the information and characteristics required to produce the product or service managed?

What method is used to monitor or, where applicable, measure the production or service planning process? (See also clause 9.1)

What are the processes in the organization's QMS that cannot be verified by inspection, measurement, or visual observation?
Examples: Welding, soldering, painting, heat treating, lamination, plating, cleaning

If the organization does not have processes in its QMS requiring validation, where is validation listed as not applicable?

Clause 8.5.2

How does the organization identify the product status with respect to inspection or monitoring requirements throughout manufacturing (or service)?

If the organization is required to provide traceability of materials or components used in manufacturing, what process does the organization use?

Clause 8.5.3

What are the materials, components, or other items provided by the organization's customers?
Examples: Raw material, test equipment, intellectual property

How does the organization control customer property?

Examples: Identify, verify, protect, safeguard, inventory

Clause 8.5.4

How does the organization ensure that materials and components are preserved during processing and delivery to its customers?

What steps are taken to protect the product during processing?

How does the organization ensure that raw materials are within the manufacturer's shelf-life warranty time?

Examples: Adhesives, sealants, coatings, paints, chemicals, solder paste/flux, desiccants

How does the organization protect the product from damage during storage?

Clause 8.5.5

What post-delivery activities are applicable to the organization?

Examples: Warranty provisions, contractual obligations (e.g., maintenance services), supplementary services (e.g., recycling or final disposal)

Clause 8.5.6

How does the organization manage changes to manufacturing processes? Customer specifications? Equipment?

How is the authority to approve changes defined?

Clause 8.6

How does the organization ensure that the customer's requirements for products are met?

What are the processes/inspections used to support the quality of product being manufactured?

Examples: Incoming material, in-process manufacturing, final release of product

What is the authorization process to approve product or services for release to customers?

Clause 8.7

How does the organization ensure that product that does not conform to product requirements is identified and controlled to prevent its unintended use or delivery?

How does the organization take action to eliminate the detected nonconformity?

How does the organization prevent the unintended use or delivery of the product?

How does the organization authorize the use, release, or acceptance of the product or service under concession by a relevant authority or the customer where applicable?

What actions are taken by the organization when the nonconforming product is detected after delivery or after use has started?

SERVICE PROVISIONS AND ISO 9001:2015

The intent of this section is to outline the application of ISO 9001:2015 to organizations engaged not in manufacturing but in providing services.

Past revisions of ISO 9001 have struggled to apply the product and manufacturing requirements of ISO to the service industry. Over the last 15 years, I have audited a wide range of organizations whose *product* was a *service*. The application of ISO 9001 to these organizations was not so difficult. I believe service-based companies have benefited from employing the discipline of ISO 9001 to their activities.

Some of the service companies I have audited include:

- A distributor of automotive components in Canada
- A distributor of fasteners in South Carolina
- A translation and software localization service in Massachusetts
- A contract custodial provider at a pharmaceutical plant in Connecticut
- An international freight forwarder at Philadelphia International Airport
- An engineering architecture firm in Kentucky
- An electrical contractor in Pennsylvania
- A project management training firm in Pennsylvania
- An ISO training provider in Connecticut
- A temporary help agency in Michigan
- A special metal importer in Florida
- An engineering/surveying company in Ireland

Of the hundreds of organizations I have audited, I recall these companies most easily—and most fondly, perhaps because of the challenge of preparing an audit plan. Many of the locations were also quite interesting. The audit at the architecture company in Kentucky included a site visit at Churchill Downs racetrack to witness the application of the firm's project planning. The site visit with the electrical contractor in Pennsylvania was at a new school being built. During the audit at the ISO training provider in Connecticut, I witnessed an internal auditor training program being conducted by the organization.

The most interesting audit was with the surveyor in Ireland. The company was contracted by the Irish government to verify that the plots of land telephone companies were using to install cell phone towers were properly mapped and owned. The government required surveyors to hold a third-party quality registration, so ISO 9001 was used. This cell tower land plot was adjacent to an ancient Irish cemetery. I used the surveyor's transit tool to verify his readings.

After a few audits of service type organizations, I realized I needed to do a better job understanding the client's processes before preparing the audit plan, so I would usually call the client and try to get a good understanding of their business model. I discovered there are five general categories of service providers: sales, distribution, engineering services, software or IT, and "other" services. Table 8.3 outlines the ISO 9001 clauses that might be relevant to each type of firm.

Table 8.3 Clause applicability for service.

#	ISO 9001:2015 clause	Sales	Distributor	Engineer	Software	Other
4	Context of the organization	Y	Y	Y	Y	Y
5	Leadership	Y	Y	Y	Y	Y
6	Planning	Y	Y	Y	Y	Y
7.1	Resources	Y	Y	Y	Y	Y
7.1.1	General	Y	Y	Y	Y	Y
7.1.2	People	Y	Y	Y	Y	Y
7.1.3	Infrastructure	M	Y	M	M	M
7.1.4	Environment for the operation of processes	N	M	M	M	N
7.1.5	Monitoring and measuring resources	M	M	M	Y	N
7.1.6	Organizational knowledge	Y	Y	Y	Y	Y
7.2	Competence	Y	Y	Y	Y	Y
7.3	Awareness	Y	Y	Y	Y	Y
7.4	Communication	Y	Y	Y	Y	Y
7.5	Documented information	Y	Y	Y	Y	Y
8.1	Operational planning and control	Y	Y	Y	Y	Y
8.2	Requirements for services	Y	Y	Y	Y	Y
8.3	Design and development services	N	N	M	Y	M
8.4	Control of externally provided services	Y	Y	M	M	M
8.5	Production and service provision					
8.5.1	Control of service provision	Y	Y	Y	Y	Y
8.5.2	Identification and traceability	Y	Y	Y	Y	M
8.5.3	Property belonging to customers	N	M	Y	Y	M
8.5.4	Preservation	Y	Y	M	Y	M
8.5.5	Post-delivery activities	Y	Y	Y	Y	M
8.5.6	Control of changes	Y	Y	Y	Y	Y
8.6	Release of products and services	Y	Y	Y	Y	Y
8.7	Control of nonconforming outputs	Y	Y	Y	Y	Y
9	Performance evaluation	Y	Y	Y	Y	Y
10	Improvement	Y	Y	Y	Y	Y

Y = yes; N = no; M = maybe

To become certified to ISO 9001:2015, all service organizations need to address the following clauses:

4	Context of the organization
5	Leadership
6	Planning
7.1.6	Organizational knowledge
7.2	Competence
7.3	Awareness
7.4	Communication
7.5	Documented information
8.2	Requirements for products and services
8.5.1	Control of production and service provision
8.5.6	Control of changes
8.6	Release of products and services
8.7	Control of nonconforming outputs
9	Performance evaluation
10	Improvement

Distributors—firms that inventory and sell products made by other companies—often have processes that closely resemble those of a manufacturing site, the major difference being that they do not make the products—they sell, purchase, store, and sometimes measure them. Some distributors provide repair or manufacturing services, so they will have requirements in production and service—possibly calibration of measuring equipment. Additionally, distributors have a warehouse. Clause 7.1.3, Infrastructure, will need to be considered in relation to transportation and information systems.

Engineering services may provide design activities such as architecture and building design, so clause 8.3, Design and development of products and services, is applicable. Software developers provide new products, so they also have requirements in clause 8.3; however, software development is quite different from hardware design, and in many cases only one individual does 90% of the work on a project. I suggest software developers consider modifying the design Stage-Gate process (Figure 8.4 in Chapter 8) to match their business model.

When considering registration to ISO 9001:2015, all service type organizations need to carefully review their processes to understand how their activities relate to identification and traceability, property belonging to customers, preservation, post-delivery activities, control of changes, release of products and services, and control of nonconforming outputs. While the jargon of software developers may be different than that of manufacturing organizations, their bugs are a type of *nonconforming product* or rejected material, and their software *releases* are similar to a hardware maker's *revision control* of a drawing. The customers provide the software developer with an electronic data file, which is *property belonging to customers* as well as intellectual property.

The service provider seeking certification to ISO 9001:2015 should review Table 8.3 with the goal of turning each "maybe" into a "yes" or "no."

To demonstrate how a service organization might approach mapping its process, the flowchart for a software developer is presented Figure 8.7.

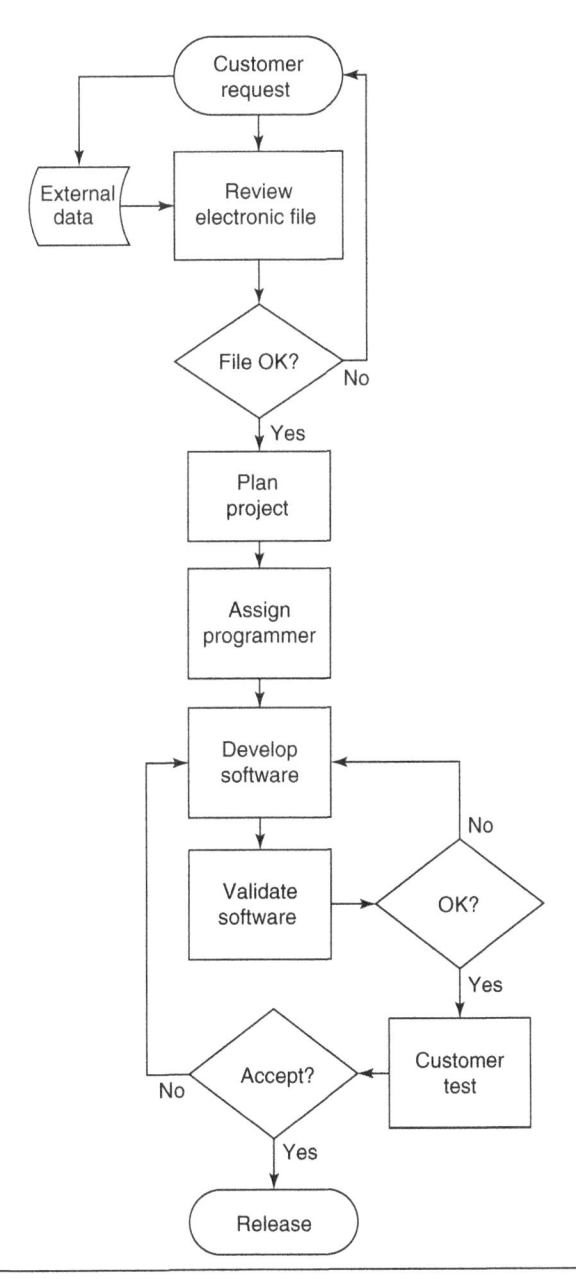

Figure 8.7 Flowchart: software developer.

The ISO 9001:2015 clauses that may apply to the software developer's processes are listed in Table 8.4. For some software developers, clause 8.5.1, Control of production and service provision, may be more applicable than clause 8.3, Design and development, as some software development can be more *process* development than *product* development. The monitoring and measuring requirement related to software development is the calibration or standardization of the hardware used to load and read the new software.

Among my service-related clients, I would say that some of the software developers effectively apply ISO 9001 to their business model, particularly companies engaged in translation or localization software. Software programmers are a unique breed: creative and often protective of their individuality. The ISO 9001 discipline has helped some software providers standardize their development process, making project transfers more efficient.

The TickIT scheme, a certification program for companies in the software development and computer industries, was based on the ISO 9001 framework. It was successfully used by many software companies. TickIT had difficulty finding auditors with sufficient IT background and was replaced by TickITplus. For more information on the TickITplus scheme, see http://www.tickitplus.org.

While several other types of service-related organizations have benefited from the application of ISO 9001, many companies using ISO 9001 certification as a marketing tool to attract new customers were disappointed that it did not generate more sales and discontinued their registration after a few years.

In the spirit of continuing improvement, service companies should establish a metric to set a baseline for improvement. Some possibilities include:

Distribution/Sales: On-time delivery, sales revenue

Software: Project cycle time, first release acceptance rate

Engineering: Performance to cost and completion time

Table 8.4 Applicable ISO 9001:2015 clauses for software developers.

Process	Applicable ISO 9001:2015 clause	Related clauses
Customer request	8.2 Requirements for services	7.5 Documented information
Review electronic file	8.5.3 Property belonging to customers	7.1.5 Monitoring and measuring
Plan project	6 Planning	
Assign programmer	7.1.2 People	7.2 Competence
Develop software	8.3 Design and development 8.5 Service provision	7.5 Documented information 8.5.2 Identification and traceability 8.5.4 Preservation 8.5.5 Post-delivery activities 8.5.6 Control of changes
Validate software	8.3 Design and development	7.1.5 Monitoring and measuring
Release product	8.6 Release of products and services	

Audit Questions

Clause 8.5.1

What are the service processes in the scope of the QMS?
Examples: Repair of equipment, distribution of product, transportation, engineering services

How does the organization provide the information and characteristics required to provide the service?

Clause 8.5.2

How does the organization identify the "product" status with respect to inspection or monitoring requirements throughout the service (if applicable)?

If the organization is required to provide traceability of materials or components used in the service, what process does the organization use?

Clause 8.5.3

What are the materials, components, or other items provided by the organization's customers?
Examples: Raw material, test equipment, intellectual property

How does the organization control customer property?
Examples: Identify, verify, protect, safeguard, inventory

Clause 8.5.4

How does the organization ensure that materials and components are preserved during processing and delivery to its customers?

What steps are taken to protect the product during processing?

How does the organization ensure that raw materials are within the manufacturer's shelf-life warranty time?
Examples: Adhesives, sealants, coatings, paints, chemicals, solder paste/flux, desiccants

How does the organization protect the product from damage during storage?

Clause 8.5.5

What post-delivery activities are applicable to the organization?
Examples: Warranty provisions, contractual obligations (e.g., maintenance services), supplementary services (e.g., recycling or final disposal)

Clause 8.5.6

How does the organization manage changes to the service processes? Customer specifications? Equipment?

How is the authority to approve changes defined?

Clause 8.6

How does the organization ensure that the customer's requirements for products (distributed) or services are met?

What are the processes/inspections used to support the quality of product being serviced?

What is the authorization process to approve product or services for release to customers?

Clause 8.7

How does the organization ensure that product or service that does not conform to requirements is identified and controlled to prevent its unintended use or delivery?

How does the organization take action to eliminate the detected nonconformity?

How does the organization prevent the unintended use or delivery of the product?

How does the organization authorize the use, release, or acceptance of the product or service under concession by a relevant authority or the customer where applicable?

What actions are taken by the organization when the nonconforming product or service is detected after delivery or after use has started?

9
Clause 9: Performance Evaluation

#	ISO 9001:2015	#	ISO 9001:2008
9	Performance evaluation	8	Measurement, analysis and improvement
9.1	Monitoring, measurement, analysis and evaluation	8.2.3	Monitoring and measurement of processes
9.1.1	General	8.2.3	Monitoring and measurement of processes
9.1.2	Customer satisfaction	8.2.1	Customer satisfaction
9.1.3	Analysis and evaluation	8.4	Analysis of data
9.2	Internal audit	8.2.2	Internal audit
9.3	Management review	5.6	Management review
9.3.1	General	5.6.1	General
9.3.2	Management review inputs	5.6.2	Review input
9.3.3	Management review outputs	5.6.3	Review output

Clause 9, Performance evaluation, is the "check" component in the PDCA process:

Check: The QMS is monitored and audited to measure performance against the organization's objectives and customer requirements. The performance and results of the QMS are reported to top management.

Clause 10, Improvement, is the "act" component:

Act: Actions are initiated to correct deficiencies and improve the quality performance as indicated by the monitoring and measurement of the QMS results. Resources and employee training are provided as appropriate to ensure improvement of the QMS.

Combining clauses 9 and 10 results in the flowchart depicted in Figure 9.1.

ISO 9001:2015 provides no new requirements—it just rearranges several requirements of ISO 9001:2008. An unfortunate change, in my opinion, is the elimination of the clause relating to the monitoring and measurement of processes. This requirement was initiated with the 2000 revision of ISO 9001 and was a major step in causing certified organizations to view their QMS as a series of processes that

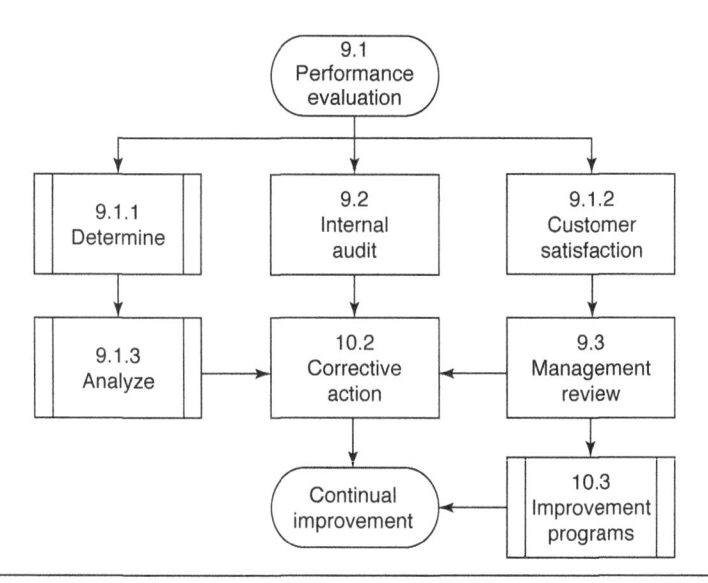

Figure 9.1 Monitor and improve.

should be monitored or measured to set a baseline for improvement. ISO 9001:2008 clause 8.2.3 stated:

> The organization shall apply suitable methods for monitoring and, where applicable, measurement of the quality management system processes. These methods shall demonstrate the ability of the processes to achieve planned results. When planned results are not achieved, correction and corrective action shall be taken, as appropriate.

This was generally interpreted by organizations and third-party auditors as requiring the organization to establish metrics (and goals) for its core processes: sales, design, purchasing, production, or service. Support processes should at a minimum be *monitored* as part of the organization's internal audit process. If the organization determined a metric was not practical or useful for a core process, then that process would also be monitored by the internal audit process. (Chapter 8 provides metric options for each core process.)

The equivalent requirements for process monitoring in ISO 9001:2015 can be found in the following clauses:

4.4 Quality management system and its processes

4.4.1: Determine and apply the criteria and methods (including monitoring, measurements and related performance indicators) needed to ensure the effective operation and control of these processes; Evaluate these processes and implement any changes needed to ensure that these processes achieve their intended results.

9.1 Monitoring, measurement, analysis and evaluation

The organization shall evaluate the performance and the effectiveness of the quality management system.

Under ISO 9001:2015, if the auditee has not established metrics for core processes, the auditor can issue a nonconformance against clause 4.4.1 for lack of defined performance indicators for sales, design, purchasing, production, or service. The auditee could assert that their performance indicators were the trend charts used to monitor sales, design, etc.—and that all were "good." With the ISO 9001:2008 requirement, "good" was not as acceptable.

Arguing with auditees (who are also your customers) is never a good thing. ISO 9001:2008 was fairly clear in its requirement to establish metrics for the core processes of an organization.

Over the last 15 years, I have been quite successful in coaching clients into establishing goals for their processes, and those goals have been helpful in measuring improvement activities. I think the writers of ISO 9001:2015 have done the ISO quality world a disservice by diluting the requirement to establish metrics and goals for core processes. It is particularly disappointing since the spirit of the 2015 standard is to promote the integration of ISO 9001 into the organization's business. Well-run businesses know all about setting hard metrics and will continue to establish metrics and goals in support of their improvement activities. Organizations seeking ISO 9001 certification for the first time should consider establishing metrics and goals for key business processes.

9.1 MONITORING, MEASUREMENT, ANALYSIS AND EVALUATION

> **9.1.1 General**
>
> The organization shall determine the methods for monitoring, measurement, analysis and evaluation of the effectiveness of the quality management system and retain appropriate documented information as evidence of the results.
>
> **9.1.2 Customer satisfaction**
>
> The organization shall determine the methods for obtaining, monitoring and reviewing customer perceptions of the degree to which their needs and expectations have been fulfilled.
>
>   NOTE: Examples of monitoring customer perceptions can include customer surveys, customer feedback on delivered products and services, meetings with customers, market-share analysis, compliments, warranty claims and dealer reports.
>
> **9.1.3 Analysis and evaluation**
>
> The organization shall analyze and evaluate:
>
> - Conformity of products and services;
> - The degree of customer satisfaction;
> - The performance and effectiveness of the quality management system;
> - Whether planning has been implemented effectively;
> - The effectiveness of actions taken to address risks and opportunities;
> - The performance of external providers;
> - The need for improvements to the quality management system.

The requirement for clause 9.1.2, Customer satisfaction, has not changed. A wide range of options can be used to obtain feedback from customers, such as:

- Customer surveys
- Supplier ratings by customers
- Customer meeting reports
- Repeat business
- Market share analysis
- Lost business analysis
- Customer compliments
- Dealer reports

Reductions in customer complaints, customer returns, and warranty returns are not sufficient measures of customer satisfaction; a proactive approach is required. Customer surveys are generally not useful in the business-to-business context. Surveys have more success (debatably) in the business-to-consumer world. I have witnessed some manufacturing organizations achieving success using surveys. It is all in the approach used—and the customer's belief that something will be done with the feedback. Some small clients use the "ad hoc" survey. When discussing a sales or technical issue with a customer, at the end of the conversation, the supplier will conduct a five-minute spot survey consisting of a few questions:

> How's our quality/delivery/support? What is working well? What's not working so well? Thank you and have a great day!

At a minimum, the organization should have a documented plan for collecting customer feedback and a file containing a record of the results. The plan should be specific, defining what the organization *will* do, not what it *may* do. Many customer feedback plans are too vague to allow auditing, as in the following example:

> The company continuously monitors customer satisfaction using a variety of monitoring and measurement methods. These include but are not limited to on-time deliveries and review and analysis of customer returns. In order to monitor customer satisfaction and perception, sales representatives, customer service representatives, and other appropriate personnel may contact customers either by phone or personal interviews.

If I were auditing this customer feedback plan, I would request to see copies of the interviews and reports from customers. If there was a reasonable number of notes—and evidence of analysis and follow-up—I would consider this organization in conformance with the requirement for customer feedback, particularly if its reject rate from customers was quite low. I would suggest that this organization modify its plan (procedure) to record the practice of collecting and recording interviews with customers and consider options to specify the type of customers interviewed (i.e., key customers) and the quantity of notes. While this approach might suit the scope and context of an organization providing machined parts, molded parts, or similar, an original equipment manufacturer or a company providing products to consumers should be more creative in soliciting feedback from customers.

In my opinion, the assessment of customer satisfaction has been a source of inconsistency on the part of ISO 9001 auditors in the past several years. Third-party auditors that issue nonconformances related to this requirement are not adding much value to the auditee's performance. The organization's response to the customer feedback nonconformance is often the implementation of a customer survey—a survey whose response rate is less than 15%. In those cases, the ISO 9001 customer satisfaction requirement is satisfied, but the organization's relationship with the customer may not improve; in fact, some customers may be annoyed by the survey!

In the spirit of ISO 9001:2015, I suggest that organizations seeking to satisfy the requirements of clause 9.1.2, Customer satisfaction, consider the *context* of their business model: What's important to their customer base? How does soliciting customer feedback fit their *business strategy*? Best-in-class organizations I've encountered in the last several years consider customer satisfaction a given for a successful business; they are seeking customer loyalty.

Clause 9.1.3, Analysis and evaluation, requires the organization to analyze and evaluate the performance of the QMS. New to **ISO 9001:2015** is the analysis of the effectiveness of actions taken to address risks and opportunities. Chapter 6 outlines risk analysis approaches available to the organization. I believe the requirement for risk analysis is a valuable addition to the new standard, particularly for smaller organizations with minimal resources. The other requirements of clause 9.1.3 will be addressed in the discussion of clause 9.3, Management review, below.

Audit Questions

Clause 9.1

What methods are used to measure the processes in the organization's QMS? What are the metrics and goals for the following processes? Sales, design, purchasing, infrastructure (maintenance), production, service

If the organization has not established a measurement for a process in the QMS, what method is used by the organization to monitor that process?

When planned results or goals are not achieved, what process is used by the organization to make corrections or take corrective action to support improvements in the QMS?

Clause 9.1.2

What are the methods or processes used by the organization to obtain feedback from customers as to the organization's performance?

Examples: Customer surveys, supplier ratings by customers, customer meeting reports, repeat business, market share analysis, lost business analysis, customer compliments, dealer reports

How or where is the process (plan) to collect the perception of customer satisfaction documented?

What records are used to verify that the customer satisfaction process is being maintained by the organization?

Clause 9.1.3

See clause 9.3, Management review.

9.2 INTERNAL AUDIT

> 9.2.1: The organization shall conduct internal audits at planned intervals to provide information on whether the quality management system is effectively implemented and maintained and conforms to the organization's own requirements for its quality management system and the requirements of this International Standard.
>
> 9.2.2: The organization shall plan, establish, implement and maintain an audit program including the frequency, methods, responsibilities, planning requirements and reporting, taking into consideration the importance of the processes concerned, changes affecting the organization and the results of previous audits. The organization shall:
>
> - Define the audit criteria and scope for each audit;
> - Select auditors and conduct audits to ensure objectivity and the impartiality of the audit process;
> - Ensure that the results of the audits are reported to relevant management;
> - Take appropriate correction and corrective action without undue delay;
> - Retain documented information as evidence of the implementation of the audit program and the audit results.

In establishing an internal audit process for the QMS, the company has several requirements to address:

- What is the schedule or audit plan?
- How is the schedule formulated?
- Have all QMS processes/clauses been audited?
- How is audit evidence obtained and recorded?
- Have the auditors been trained/qualified?
- Are audits occurring according to schedule?
- Are the follow-up actions and reporting to management timely?

For an organization seeking registration to ISO 9001:2015 for the first time, evidence should be provided that the organization conducted an internal audit to all clauses in ISO 9001:2015. The internal audit results should provide "information on whether the quality management system . . . conforms to . . . the requirements of this International Standard." Additionally, the organization needs to demonstrate that it "conforms to the organization's own requirements for its quality management system." To satisfy this requirement, internal audit evidence must show that the organization's practices match its interpretation of ISO 9001:2015 as well as its related documented information (procedures and instructions).

Table 9.1 shows a process audit plan for the Jones Plastics Company, the injection molding company from Chapter 4. Jones Co. performs the manufacturing processes of molding, machining, and assembly using customer-provided designs.

This plan is based on the process audit approach. When auditing a core process such as sales or production, the related support processes can also be sampled. Support processes that connect to all core processes are documents and records,

Table 9.1 Internal audit plan for a process-based audit.

Process	Impact	Frequency	Scope	Leadership	Objectives	Competence	Documents	Requirements	Design	Purchasing	Production	Inspection	Identification	Preservation	Calibration	Maintenance	Work Env.	Shipping	Performance	Improvement
Core									NA											
Sales	L	18			x	x	x	x												
Design	NA	–																		
Purchasing	L	18			x	x	x			x										
Engineering	L	18			x	x	x				x	x	x	x	x					
Molding	H	6			x	x	x				x	x	x	x	x	x	x			
Machining	M	12			x	x	x				x	x	x	x	x	x	x			
Assembly	M	12			x	x	x				x	x	x	x	x	x	x	x		
Shipping	L	18			x	x	x													
Support																				
Management responsibilities	L	18	x	x	x		x												x	x
Quality management	M	12	x				x									x			x	x
Human resources	L	18				x	x													
Facilities management	M	12				x	x									x	x	x		

communication of the quality policy and quality objectives, and competence and training. Production and service processes will typically also link to calibration, maintenance, and work environment factors. The ISO 9001:2015 clauses at the top of the plan are listed in generic terms to simplify explanation of the process audit concept. In practice, the organization will need to connect the generic ISO 9001 clauses to the actual terms of ISO 9001:2015 to ensure that all requirements are audited. In planning internal audits, the organization needs to satisfy the requirement of clause 9.2.2:

> The organization shall plan, establish, implement and maintain an audit program including the frequency, methods, responsibilities, planning requirements and reporting, taking into consideration the importance of the processes concerned, changes affecting the organization and the results of previous audits.

The organization should establish a priority system for allotting auditor time in order to maximize information gleaned from the internal audits. Processes with deficiencies from past audits may need to be audited more frequently than audits with no issues. Processes presenting the greatest risk to the organization (e.g., customer returns, cost impact) should also receive more auditing attention. In the audit plan shown in Table 9.1, the Jones Plastics Company established a ranking system whereby processes with a high impact should be audited every 6 months; medium impact, every 12 months; and low impact, every 18 months. Once the plan is organized for impact and frequency, the organization should assign auditors for the next year or two.

Qualifications and Training Requirements for Internal Auditors

Clause 9.2 does not explicitly define a requirement for auditor qualifications. It does state: "Select auditors and conduct audits to ensure objectivity and the impartiality of the audit process." This is common practice in auditing for all management systems. An internal auditor from the production process should not be assigned to audit his or her own process. Those assigned the responsibility and authority to manage the QMS need to be judicious when deciding whether they are too involved in providing internal audits for the clause they are responsible for managing.

Clause 7.2, Competence, states: "The organization shall ensure that these persons are competent on the basis of appropriate education, training or experience." An experienced third-party auditor will challenge the organization on how and why the organization's internal auditors are qualified to conduct ISO 9001:2015 internal audits. A recommended approach for qualifying internal auditors is to have several employees (depending on the size of organization) trained by a QMS expert, either through a public training course or on site if that option is more efficient due to class size. Once a few employees are qualified to conduct ISO 9001 internal audits, the organization can have them train other employees to do the same. It is important to have a defined plan for qualifying auditors—and to keep records of how they are trained. If a third-party consultant is used to conduct internal audits, their qualifications should be noted in the organization's files, and their role should be documented in the organization's procedures.

There are a few ways an organization may *retain documented information as evidence of the implementation of the audit program and the audit results.* Prepared check sheets or customized question lists are commonly used to drive the audit fact finding. One option used by both internal and external auditors is the process diagram or "turtle diagram," an example of which is shown in Figure 9.2. The

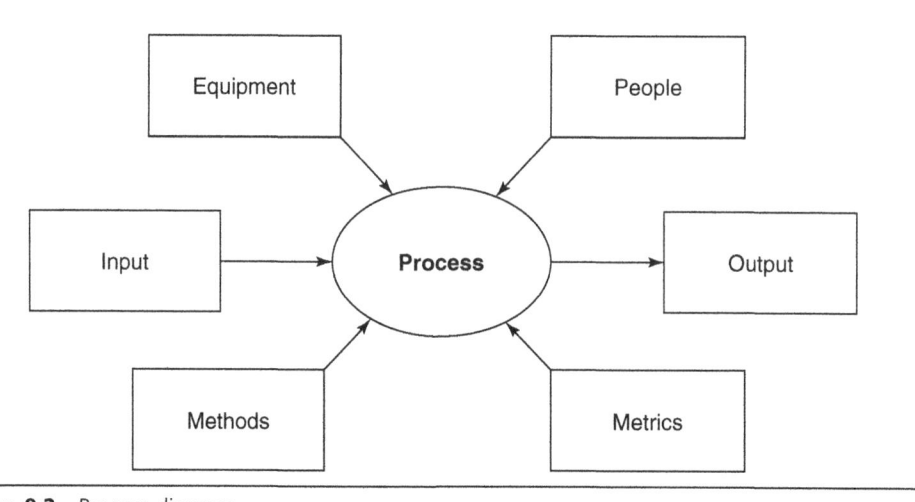

Figure 9.2 Process diagram.

auditor uses this type of diagram to collect and record input and output data for a process in the "head" and "tail," while the four "legs" capture the related equipment, machines, and measuring devices; the employees involved (training); the process metrics or measures; and the methods or procedures defining the process and controls.

While the process diagram can be used effectively to collect evidence during an audit, this technique is prone to error if the auditor is not properly trained and the person being interviewed does not understand the terms and the questions being asked. I think the process diagram is best used in preparing for an audit—and should be supplemented with conventional check sheets during the actual audit and interviews. Figure 9.3 shows a process diagram for the audit of an injection molding process.

Prior to interviewing the operating personnel, the auditor should meet with various personnel involved in the process planning and collect information on the inputs, raw materials, etc. The support documentation to control the process, the specific equipment involved, and the parameters to measure the effectiveness of the process are researched and recorded by the auditor. The employees involved in supporting the process being audited are identified as well. This information assists the auditor in verifying the training required for operations, quality, and maintenance personnel. Finally, the output of the process provides the auditor with information on quality acceptance criteria and lot quantities.

An audit check sheet can then be used to control the interviews during the audit. In a production or service operation, the check sheet can be organized as process based to combine several clauses of ISO 9001:2015. An example of a check sheet for a production process is shown in Figure 9.4.

Internal Audit Reports and Follow-Up Actions

The organization needs to maintain a report of the results of the internal audit, including a summary report defining how the audit was conducted, issues raised (nonconformances and opportunities for improvement [OFIs]), and follow-up

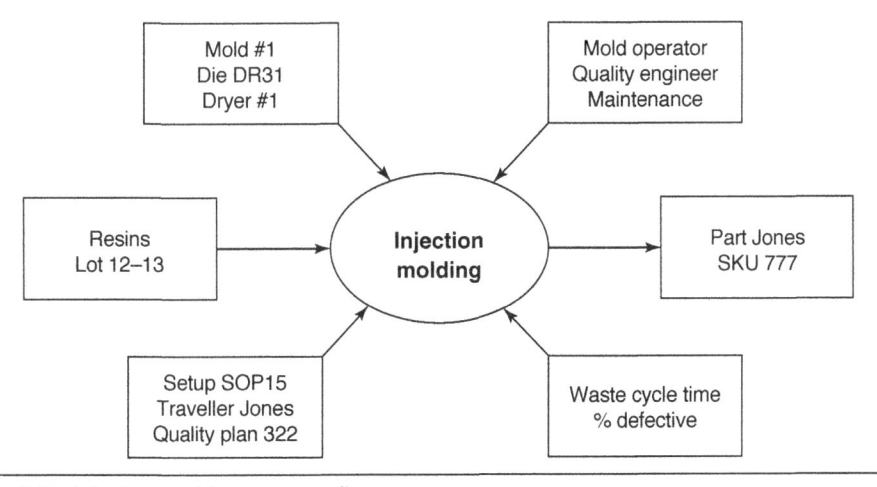

Figure 9.3 Injection molding process diagram.

Process: Production and service provision	Clause: 8.5
Date: _____	
Auditor: _____	Auditees: _____

C = conforming; NC = nonconforming; O = Opportunity

Interview a few production employees to verify that the processes used to manufacture the product match the production plans	**Location/name of equipment:** **Employee name(s):**
Review information being used: • Instructions/drawings for the product? • Revisions correct? • Prior operations are approved? • Product and materials identified? • Traceability (8.5.2)?	
Review quality inspections (8.6): • Raw material approval • 1st article • In-process • Release to next process Witness inspection process, if applicable	
Review inspection devices (7.1.5.2): • Device identification? • Calibrations current?	List here and verify in section 7.1.5.2
Review process used when product measured does not meet the inspection specification (8.7.1)	Record under section 8.7.1
Review process used for preventive maintenance (7.1.3) • Equipment operator • Maintenance department • Safety devices	Record under section 7.1.3
Review training records for employee (7.2) (record names for audit of training)	Record under section 7.2
Review employee's knowledge of: • Quality policy (5.2) • Quality objectives (7.2) • How quality policy and objectives relate to employee	
Review the process the employee uses to suggest improvements to this operation (10.3)	
Comments/NCs/opportunities:	

Figure 9.4 Sample check sheet for clause 8.5, Production and service provision.

activities defined. Nonconformances should be entered in the organization's corrective action process. OFIs should be addressed by the organization, with follow-up response documented. An OFI is generally defined as an observation, which is not a nonconformance but a suggestion to improve the efficiency, clarity, or some other aspect of the process. These opportunities should be recorded in the final audit report for the benefit of the organization.

> **Audit Questions**
>
> **Clause 9.2.1**
>
> *How does the organization plan and schedule internal audits of the QMS?*
>
> *How does the organization record discrepancies or nonconformities (findings) discovered when conducting internal audits of the QMS?*
>
> *How does the organization use the status and importance of the processes in the QMS in establishing audit frequency?*
>
> *How does the organization use the results of previous audits of the QMS in establishing audit frequency?*
>
> *How are the internal auditors trained and qualified to perform internal audits?*
>
> *How does the organization ensure that internal audits are conducted with objectivity and impartiality?*
>
> *If internal audits are conducted by a third-party auditor, is the auditor qualified to perform audits to ISO 9001:2015?*
>
> *If internal audits are conducted by a third-party auditor, has the organization's management approved the audit plan and the process for follow-up activities?*

9.3 MANAGEMENT REVIEW

> **9.3.1 General**
>
> Top management shall review the organization's quality management system, at planned intervals, to ensure its continuing suitability, adequacy, effectiveness and **alignment with the strategic direction of the organization.**
>
> **9.3.2 Management review inputs**
>
> The management review shall be planned and carried out taking into consideration:
>
> - The status of actions from previous management reviews;
> - **Changes in external and internal issues that are relevant to the quality management system;**
> - The adequacy of resources;
> - The effectiveness of actions taken to address risks and opportunities;
> - Opportunities for improvement.
>
> The management review shall contain information on the performance and effectiveness of the quality management system, including trends in:
>
> - Customer satisfaction and feedback from relevant interested parties;
> - The extent to which quality objectives have been met;
> - Process performance and conformity of products and services;

- Nonconformities and corrective actions;
- Monitoring and measurement results;
- Audit results;
- The performance of external providers.

9.3.3 Management review outputs

The outputs of the management review shall include decisions and actions related to:

- Opportunities for improvement;
- Any need for changes to the quality management system;
- Resource needs.

The organization shall retain documented information as evidence of the results of management reviews.

The organization has several options related to reporting the status of the QMS. The management review meeting can be incorporated into the organization's business management meetings. Whatever the format, the agenda of the QMS review meeting is straightforward and prescriptive—each agenda topic needs to be addressed during the frequency cycle established in the organization's planning. At a minimum, the QMS should be reviewed annually by the organization's senior staff.

Consistent with the requirement of ISO 9001:2015 clause 5.1, Leadership and commitment ("ensuring the integration of the quality management system requirements into the organization's business processes"), top management should both attend and fully participate in the quality management meetings. The emphasis on top management's stronger involvement in the QMS is new to **ISO 9001:2015**. Many ISO 9001–certified organizations have already integrated quality management into their business model and strategy. I have audited companies of all sizes whose quality performance metrics were woven into the business plan: the KPIs assigned to quality and business parameters also included the environmental metrics of hazardous waste reduction, material recycling, and utility use. Quality waste reduction projects included improved environmental performance.

In my observations, best-in-class organizations have established a BMS incorporating their financial, quality, safety, and environmental systems into a cohesive operational model. A natural byproduct of a successful BMS is improved employee, supplier, and community relationships. Unfortunately, I have also audited too many ISO 9001–certified organizations where top management treats their ISO 9001 certificate as "just another program," with responsibilities delegated and managed with the least drain on resources and costs. ISO 9001:2015 is attempting to address this apparent gap by providing the registrar's third-party auditors with clear requirements related to top management's direct involvement in the organization's quality performance and connection to the organization's business strategy.

"Suitability" means the QMS must be appropriate to the organization's current processes—what the organization does. If the organization adds new manufacturing or service activities, the organization needs to consider whether the QMS is still appropriate. "Adequacy" refers to whether the QMS meets the requirements of the International Standard and is implemented appropriately. "Effectiveness" refers to whether it is achieving the desired results (i.e., meeting its objectives). When reviewing the QMS, management should provide a summary statement addressing the suitability, adequacy, and effectiveness of the QMS, highlighting where gaps may exist and where management actions (and resources) are required to put the quality commitments back on track.

> **Audit Questions**
>
> **Clause 9.3.1**
>
> *What is the frequency for conducting management reviews of the QMS? What are the dates of the two most recent meetings?*
>
> *How does the organization review the performance of the products (or services) provided by the organization?*
>
> *How does the organization review the performance of the processes in the QMS?*
>
> Examples: Sales/order entry, design, external providers (purchasing), manufacturing, services, engineering support, quality assurance, facilities/maintenance, shipping/warehouse, human resources
>
> *Do management review notes contain information on:*
>
> - Results of audits?
> - Customer feedback?
> - Status of corrective actions?
> - Follow-up actions from previous management reviews?
> - Changes that could affect the QMS?
>
> *How does the organization summarize the suitability, adequacy, and effectiveness of its QMS?*

10
Clause 10: Improvement

#	ISO 9001:2015	#	ISO 9001:2008
10	Improvement	8.5	Improvement
10.1	General	8.5.1	Continual improvement
10.2	Nonconformity and corrective action	8.5.2	Corrective action
10.3	Continual improvement	8.5.1	Continual improvement

10.1 GENERAL

> The organization shall determine and select opportunities for improving the performance and effectiveness of the quality management system and implement any necessary actions to enhance customer satisfaction to include:
>
> - Improving products and services to meet requirements as well as to address future needs and expectations;
> - Correcting, preventing or reducing undesired effect.

Clause 10 requires the organization to establish and maintain processes to correct errors and make improvements in the QMS. In addition to ensuring that the organization complies with its customer commitments, the ISO 9001:2015 standard requires the organization to analyze and improve its performance. Prior versions of ISO 9001 included clause 8.5.3, Preventive action:

> The organization shall determine action to eliminate the causes of potential nonconformities in order to prevent their occurrence. Preventive actions shall be appropriate to the effects of the potential problems.

The risk analysis clauses of ISO 9001:2015 outline a form of preventive action; the entire QMS is preventive in nature. The removal of the preventive action requirement is long overdue. Readers with many years of experience with ISO 9001 auditing will be relieved to no longer hear an auditor say "You don't have any preventive actions" or "That's a corrective action, not a preventive action." The advent of Six Sigma and lean manufacturing in the last several years has provided organizations of all sizes with techniques to eliminate the causes of potential nonconformities. Proper application of risk analysis is a good addition to ISO 9001, in my opinion.

10.2 NONCONFORMITY AND CORRECTIVE ACTION

> 10.2.1: When nonconformity occurs, including any arising from complaints, the organization shall react to the nonconformity and, as applicable, take action to control and correct and deal with the consequences.
>
> The organization shall evaluate the need for action to eliminate the cause of the nonconformity, in order that it does not recur or occur elsewhere, by:
>
> - Reviewing and analyzing the nonconformity;
> - Determining the causes of the nonconformity;
> - Determining if similar nonconformities exist, or could potentially occur;
> - Implementing any action needed;
> - Reviewing the effectiveness of any corrective action taken;
> - Updating the risks and opportunities determined during planning, if necessary;
> - Making changes to the QMS, if necessary.
>
> Corrective actions shall be appropriate to the effects of the nonconformities encountered.
>
> 10.2.2: The organization shall retain documented information as evidence of the nature of the nonconformities and any subsequent actions taken and the results of any corrective action.

Most companies, whether they have a formal QMS or not, have a corrective action process. For over 25 years, ISO 9001 has promulgated corrective action initiatives, which, in my opinion, has made a great contribution to improvements in manufacturing product quality and services.

Some situations call for a formal, multifunction corrective action with cause analysis, effectiveness monitoring, and so forth, but a find-and-fix approach can often be effective as well. During a plant tour, several minor deficiencies might be observed. In that case, rather than entering the items in the corrective action program, the issues could be fixed or resolved and recorded in a log such as the one shown in Table 10.1.

The log would be reviewed by the quality manager (or team) to ensure proper follow-up. If the issues recurred, a formal nonconformance/corrective action might be necessary.

Table 10.1 Examples of find-and-fix corrective actions.

August 1, 2015, plant inspection	Responsible	Fix	Follow-up	Date closed
Parts in machine shop not identified	John	Added hold tag	Review next audit	8/5/15
Obsolete instruction near mold machine	Mike	Removed	Discuss with mold supervisor	8/2/15
(2) Scales at loading dock missing inspection sticker	Mike	Review with QC	Issue corrective action	Open

If the situation requires the issuance of a corrective action, the action should not only fix the problem but also maximize analysis to prevent recurrence of the issue. In a corrective action the actions should correct the situation, provide analysis of cause, and provide correction for cause. The following is an example of a corrective action:

Description of Nonconformity

Scales at loading dock not calibrated

Corrective Action

Calibrate scales

Root Cause

The manual Master Calibration list is not being maintained

Correction for Cause

Quality manager will purchase new software system with schedule capability

Diligence in both root cause analysis and determining the correction for cause is essential in maintaining an effective corrective action process. A common root cause analysis technique referred to as Five Whys involves questioning what caused a problem until you can no longer answer why something happened. See Appendix D for an example of Five Whys. For example:

A car crashes into a store. Why? The gas pedal stuck. Why? Something got in the way. Why? The floor mat moved. Why? It wasn't properly secured. Why? The attachment design did not work. Why? It was either incorrectly installed or poorly designed. Why? I give up! Ask the car manufacturer.

One of my colleagues in the quality world claims there are only two root causes for every defect in manufacturing: incompetent workers and arrogant management. And actually, he would say, "the workers are incompetent because management is arrogant!" In reality there are several general categories of reasons for failures in manufacturing and services:

- Misunderstanding of customer requirements
- Poor design
- Lack of clear instructions
- Supplier error
- Human error (training)

When the root cause is determined to be human error, or lack of training, the risk of the problem reoccurring is usually high. If the organization does not make a major upgrade to its training program, then the *correction for cause* was not effective. Most third-party auditors are reluctant to accept human error or lack of training as a root cause. There is almost always an attendant cause when human error occurs, such as unclear or complicated instructions.

To ensure that corrections resolve the issues, and thus avoid repeating the corrective action review and change steps, the organization should establish effectiveness measures. Using the above scale calibration example, the organization would increase the sampling frequency for calibration checks—or better yet, ask the users of calibrated devices to take ownership of the status of devices in their area. Most third-party auditors spend considerable time reviewing the organization's corrective actions and follow-up activities to evaluate whether corrections are completed in a timely fashion and the fixes are effective.

> **Audit Questions**
>
> **Clause 10.2**
>
> *How does the organization respond to:*
>
> - Customer complaints?
> - Returned products from customers?
> - Defective product or material from suppliers?
> - Defective material or product during manufacturing?
> - Nonconformances noted during internal audits?
> - Nonconformances noted during customer or third-party audits?
>
> *Does the corrective action process include:*
>
> - Correcting the nonconformance?
> - Determining the cause of the nonconformance?
> - Providing a correction for the cause to prevent reoccurrence?
> - Reviewing the effectiveness of the corrective action taken?
> - Closing corrective actions as planned?

10.3 CONTINUAL IMPROVEMENT

> The organization shall continually improve the suitability, adequacy and effectiveness of the quality management system.
>   The organization shall consider the results of analysis and evaluation, and the outputs from management review, to determine if there are needs or opportunities that shall be addressed as part of continual improvement.

The trends in causes of corrective actions in an organization can indicate the need for improvements. If there are continual or systemic issues related to weak or poorly implemented design projects, the organization could establish an improvement team to improve the design process. Many organizations are using quality tools such as Six Sigma to bring about improvements. Six Sigma is:

> A method that provides organizations tools to improve the capability of their business processes. This increase in performance and decrease in process variation lead to defect reduction and improvement in profits, employee morale, and quality of products or services. Six Sigma quality is

a term generally used to indicate a process is well controlled (within process limits ±3s from the center line in a control chart, and requirements/tolerance limits ±6s from the center line). (Kubiak and Benbow 2009, 6–7)

ASQ's website (www.asq.org) has many resources for organizations interested in learning more about Six Sigma. Appendix E summarizes Six Sigma. A scaled-down version of Six Sigma used by many companies to support their improvement efforts is the DMAIC process. The following is a summary of the DMAIC process:

DMAIC is a data-driven quality strategy used to improve processes. It is an integral part of a Six Sigma initiative, but in general can be implemented as a standalone quality improvement procedure or as part of other process improvement initiatives such as lean. DMAIC is an acronym for the five phases that make up the process:

- *Define* the problem, improvement activity, opportunity for improvement, the project goals, and customer (internal and external) requirements.
- *Measure* process performance.
- *Analyze* the process to determine root causes of variation, poor performance (defects).
- *Improve* process performance by addressing and eliminating the root causes.
- *Control* the improved process and future process performance.

The DMAIC process easily lends itself to the project approach to quality improvement encouraged and promoted by Juran. (Borror 2009, 333)

I've seen many small organizations become proficient in utilizing the DMAIC process to bring about improvements in many facets of their business. Increased material utilization, reduction of product defects, and reduction of cycle time in software development are examples of where the DMAIC process can be effective. The discipline of ISO 9001 controls is quite consistent with DMAIC steps and the improvements obtained should be maintained as elements of the QMS.

Other quality tools such as lean manufacturing can be utilized to improve the efficiency of processes and productivity. According to ASQ:

Lean manufacturing is a system of techniques and activities for running a manufacturing or service operation. The techniques and activities differ according to the application at hand but they have the same underlying principle: the elimination of all non-value-adding activities and waste from the business.

Lean techniques can be very helpful in reducing setup time, reorganizing the plant floor, and removing waste. Employees generally appreciate the lean process as the improvements occur rather quickly and make their jobs easier. Appendix F summarizes Lean.

DMAIC and lean manufacturing programs, implemented in conjunction with an ISO 9001 certification, provide an organization with terrific tools to improve their business results.

Audit Questions

Clause 10.3

How does the organization improve the performance of the organization's QMS:

- Improvement teams?
- Projects?
- Trend charts?

What examples indicate improvement?

11
Interpretation Guidance: ISO 9001:2015 Standard

Several clauses of ISO 9001:2015 contain requirements that, in my opinion, are difficult to interpret, and Annex A, *Clarification of new structure, terminology and concepts*, does not effectively clarify them. This chapter discusses some of the clauses that I believe could be clearer in defining auditable requirements.

CLAUSE 6.1, ACTIONS TO ADDRESS RISKS AND OPPORTUNITIES

Clause 6.1 includes references to previous clause requirements using the clause number only, without clarifying the linkage. Organizations or auditors should not have to return to clauses 4.1, 4.2, and 4.4 to understand the issues or requirements connected to clause 6.1, or why these clauses are important in the context of planning for risks.

6.1 Actions to address risks and opportunities (ASQ/ANSI/ISO 9001:2015, as released October 2015)

6.1.1 When planning for the quality management system, the organization shall consider the issues referred to in **4.1** and the requirements referred to in **4.2** and determine the risks and opportunities that need to be addressed to:

a) give assurance that the quality management system can achieve its intended result(s);

b) enhance desirable effects;

c) prevent, or reduce, undesired effects;

d) achieve improvement

6.1.2 The organization shall plan:

a) actions to address these risks and opportunities;

b) how to:

1) integrate and implement the actions into its quality management system processes (see **4.4**);

2) evaluate the effectiveness of these actions

Actions taken to address risks and opportunities shall be proportionate to the potential impact on the conformity of products and services.

NOTE 1 Options to address risks can include avoiding risk, taking risk in order to pursue an opportunity, eliminating the risk source, changing the likelihood or consequences, sharing the risk, or retaining risk by informed decision.

NOTE 2 Opportunities can lead to the adoption of new practices, launching new products, opening new markets, addressing new clients, building partnerships, using new technology and other desirable and viable possibilities to address the organization's or its customers' needs.

In Chapter 6, I paraphrased this clause to directly describe the linkage with clause 4.1, Understanding the organization and its context; clause 4.2, Understanding the needs and expectations of interested parties; and clause 4.4, Quality management system and its processes. I believe the paraphrased clause 6.1 more clearly defines the actions required to address risks and opportunities:

6.1 Actions to address risks and opportunities (Author's paraphrase)

6.1.1 When planning for the quality management system, the organization shall consider the **context of the organization and the needs of interested parties**.

The organization shall determine the risks and opportunities that need to be addressed to give assurance that the quality management system can:

- Achieve its intended results;
- Enhance desirable effects;
- Prevent, or reduce, undesired effects;
- Achieve improvement.

6.1.2 The organization shall plan:

- Actions to address these risks and opportunities;
- How to integrate and implement the actions into its quality management system processes;
- How to evaluate the effectiveness of these actions.

Actions taken to address risks and opportunities shall be proportionate to the potential impact on the conformity of products and services.

Clause 6.1 includes five levels of indexing (6.1.2.a, 1). Why is this necessary? The paraphrased clause 6.1 in the *Handbook* eliminates the fifth level—and could have been just as clear with three levels. The previous revision of ISO 9001 in 2008 used a maximum of three levels and is much more readable and easier to interpret than the 2015 version. Other clauses in ISO 9001:2015 that use excessive indexing include clauses 8.1 Operational planning and control, 8.5 Production and service provision, and 9.2 Internal audit.

Writers of the 2015 standard may defend the need to provide multiple levels for a requirement to facilitate the clear presentation of gaps or nonconformances in an organization's actions related to the requirement. This is contradicted by the majority of the clauses in ISO 9001:2015. For example, clause 8.5.2, Identification and traceability, contains four requirements ("shall"s) but has no indexing:

8.5.2 Identification and traceability

The organization shall use suitable means to identify outputs when it is necessary to ensure the conformity of products and services.

The organization shall identify the status of outputs with respect to monitoring and measurement requirements throughout production and service provision.

The organization shall control the unique identification of the outputs when traceability is a requirement, and shall retain the documented information necessary to enable traceability.

Clause 8.5.3, Property belonging to customers or external providers, and clause 8.5.4, Preservation, are also not excessively indexed. Ironically, in my mind, these clauses have more potential for discrepancies and nonconformances than the overindexed clause 6.1.

Section A4, *Clarification of new structure, terminology and concepts*, is intended to clarify the requirements of clause 6.1, Actions to address risks and opportunities. The clarification provides a path for organizations to essentially ignore the new requirement related to analyzing and addressing risk, as it indicates that risk planning documentation is not required:

A4 Risk-based thinking

Although (6.1) specifies that the organization shall plan actions to address risks, **there is no requirement for formal methods for risk management or a documented risk management process**. Organizations can decide whether or not to develop a more extensive risk management methodology than is required by this International Standard, e.g. through the application of other guidance or standards.

Not all the processes of a quality management system represent the same level of risk in terms of the organization's ability to meet its objectives, and the effects of uncertainty are not the same for all organizations. Under the requirements of 6.1 the organization is responsible for its application of risk-based thinking and the actions it takes to address risk, including whether or not to retain documented information as evidence of its determination of risks.

The paraphrased interpretation in the *Handbook* indicates there is a requirement for the organization to "determine the risks and opportunities that need to be addressed to give assurance that the quality management system can achieve its intended results." I believe many third-party auditors will agree with this interpretation of clause 6.1.1 and will expect some form of documentation showing that risk-based thinking is part of the organization's QMS. Again, A4, Risk-based thinking, states:

Under the requirements of 6.1 the organization is responsible for its application of risk-based thinking and the actions it takes to address risk, including whether or not to retain documented information as evidence of its determination of risks.

A guideline I use in training internal auditors is, "If it is not documented, it didn't happen." An auditor having to determine if an organization is applying risk-based thinking without objective evidence (documentation) is contrary to the concept of auditing. Since the genesis of ISO 9000 in 1987, anecdotal or verbal evidence has never been acceptable verification for satisfying a requirement.

Providing evidence that the organization assesses the risks and opportunities related to its purpose, business strategy, and expectations of interested parties to ensure that the QMS meets its objectives should be a requirement, unless *after consideration* the organization can convince themselves (and the auditor) that the risk analysis process adds no value to their business—which is unlikely, in my opinion. Even very small organizations have reason to be concerned about the challenges and risks facing their business.

In my opinion, the elimination of the preventive action requirement is a good step. The advent of the Six Sigma and lean manufacturing quality tools in the last several years has provided organizations of all sizes with techniques to eliminate the causes of potential nonconformances. Quality tools currently used in many organizations include strategic planning process, SWOT analysis, Six Sigma, and lean manufacturing programs. FMEA could be applied. While organizations with an effective QMS certainly understand the risks related to their operations, the new requirements of ISO 9001:2015 may have a positive effect on organizations by requiring a more formalized risk evaluation process and subjecting it to a third-party audit. I encourage organizations certifying to ISO 9001:2015 to include some form of documentation explaining their risk planning process. It is a good business practice—and may help the organization avoid a disagreement with an auditor who did not read Annex 4!

A1 STRUCTURE AND TERMINOLOGY

ISO 9001:2015 includes several changes in terminology. "Documented information" now includes documents, procedures, and work instructions as well as quality records. Annex A section A1 explains:

> **A1 Structure and terminology**
>
> The clause structure (i.e. clause sequence) and some of the terminology of this edition of this International Standard, in comparison with the previous edition (ISO 9001:2008), have been changed to improve alignment with other management systems standards.
>
> **There is no requirement in this International Standard** for its structure and terminology to be applied to the documented information of an organization's quality management system.
>
> The structure of clauses is intended to provide a coherent presentation of requirements, rather than a model for documenting an organization's policies, objectives and processes. The structure and content of documented information related to a quality management system can often be more relevant to its users if it relates to both the processes operated by the organization and information maintained for other purposes.
>
> **There is no requirement** for the terms used by an organization to be replaced by the terms used in this International Standard to specify quality

management system requirements. Organizations can choose to use terms which suit their operations (e.g. using "records," "documentation" or "protocols" rather than "documented information"; or "supplier," "partner" or "vendor" rather than "external provider"). Table A.1 [Table 11.1] shows the major differences in terminology between this edition of this International Standard and the previous edition.

According to A1, Structure and terminology, the clause structure was changed from ISO 9001:2008 to improve alignment with other management system standards. I am quite familiar with the environmental management standard ISO 14001:2015; that standard has the same changes in structure and terminology. It also has the same caveat as ISO 9001: there is no need to adopt the new terminology. The justification for this change is quite weak, particularly with the dilution of the concept of records. As described earlier in the *Handbook*, quality records are an important part of the QMS. In addition to providing evidence of conformance to a specification or requirement, a quality record can often be an organization's best defense against a customer product return or even a lawsuit. Chapter 7 provides information on the recommended approach to managing quality records.

The Annex provides further guidance on documented information:

A6 Documented information

As part of the alignment with other management system standards, a common clause on "documented information" has been adopted without significant change or addition (see 7.5.). Where appropriate, text elsewhere in this International Standard has been aligned with its requirements. Consequently, "documented information" is used for all document requirements.

Where ISO 9001:2008 used specific terminology such as "document" or "documented procedures," "quality manual" or "quality plan," this edition of this International Standard defines requirements to "maintain documented information."

Table 11.1 Terminology differences between ISO 9001:2008 and ISO 9001:2015.

ISO 9001:2008	ISO 9001:2015
Products	Products and services
Exclusions	Not used (see section A5 for clarification of applicability)
Management representative	Not used (similar responsibilities and authorities are assigned but there is no requirement for a single management representative)
Documentation, quality manual, documented procedures, records	Documented information
Work environment	Environment for the operation of processes
Monitoring and measuring equipment	Monitoring and measuring resources
Purchased product	Externally provided products and services
Supplier	External provider

Where ISO 9001:2008 used the term "records" to denote documents needed to provide evidence of conformity with requirements, this is now expressed as a requirement to "retain documented information." The organization is responsible for determining what documented information needs to be retained, the period of time for which it is to be retained and the media to be used for its retention.

A requirement to "maintain" documented information does not exclude the possibility that the organization might also need to "retain" that same documented information for a particular purpose, e.g. to retain previous versions of it.

Where this International Standard refers to "information" rather than "documented information" (e.g. in 4.1: "The organization shall monitor and review the information about these external and internal issues"), there is no requirement that this information is to be documented. In such situations, the organization can decide whether or not it is necessary or appropriate to maintain documented information.

ISO 9001:2015 does not explicitly refer to the requirement for a quality manual; in fact, A6 guidance allows organizations more latitude in determining what requires documentation. An experienced third-party auditor, when assessing how management reviewed the information about external and internal issues, will expect to see some form of written report—not "controlled," but documented and dated. As stated previously, a verbal discussion will not suffice for most auditors.

My recommendations in the *Handbook* suggest that organizations currently maintaining a quality manual should continue using it as a high-level consolidation of the key elements—or road map—of their quality documentation (as was required by ISO 9001:2008). Organizations whose quality manual paraphrases each ISO 9001 clause requirement—going back through several ISO 9001 revisions—should seriously consider updating their quality manual to include:

- A description of the organization's business model, including the context of the organization and the expectations of interested parties

- The scope (the activities, processes, and buildings and locations) of the QMS

- A description of those ISO 9001:2015 requirements that are not applicable to the QMS, as they do not affect the organization's ability or responsibility to ensure the conformity of its products and services

- The documented procedures (documented information) established for the QMS, or reference to them

- A description of the QMS processes and how they interact

- The quality policy

- Responsibilities/authorities

As an RABQSA (Exemplar Global) qualified lead auditor (QMS, EMS) for almost 20 years and having conducted hundreds of audits for companies ranging from a few employees to thousands of employees, I cannot understand what the authors of Annex A were trying to promulgate with the "new" documented information concept. The third paragraph in A1 Structure and terminology states:

The structure of clauses is intended to provide a coherent presentation of requirements, rather than a model for documenting an organization's policies, objectives and processes. The structure and content of documented information related to a quality management system can often be more relevant to its users if it relates to both the processes operated by the organization and information maintained for other purposes.

It is not clear to me how an organization would find ways to apply the "advice" given in the above statement. I suggest organizations continue to "document what you do—do what you document." The documentation of the QMS should be suitable to the organization's business and provide value in managing the organization's processes. The overarching principle in documentation should be to formalize what is needed to ensure that users of the documentation have a source for information and instructions that is accurate and timely, providing consistency in managing the business.

Appendix A
ISO 9001:2015 Gap Analysis
Summary of Changes from ISO 9001:2008

ISO 9001 CHRONOLOGY

1987	ISO 9001 initial issue
1994	ISO 9001 revision
2000	ISO 9001 revision
2008	ISO 9001 amendment
2015	ISO 9001 revision

ISO 9001:2015 AS A PROCESS

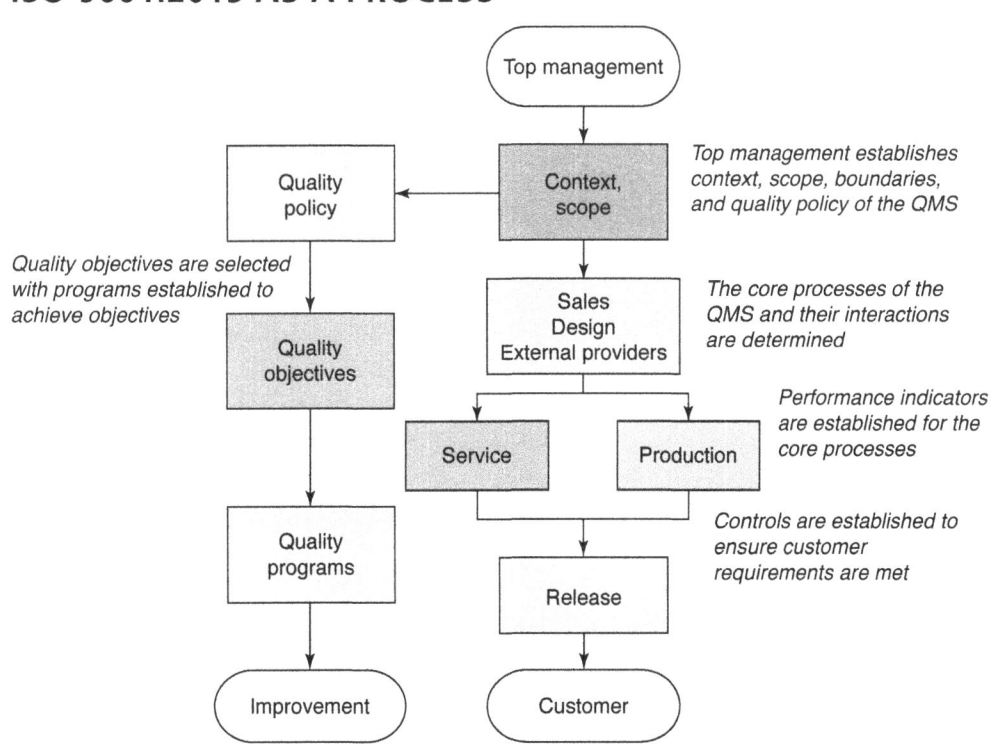

Top management establishes context, scope, boundaries, and quality policy of the QMS

Quality objectives are selected with programs established to achieve objectives

The core processes of the QMS and their interactions are determined

Performance indicators are established for the core processes

Controls are established to ensure customer requirements are met

Support processes: Documentation, communication, training, quality assurance, calibration, maintenance, corrective action, internal audit, risk assessment, monitoring and measurement, management responsibilities, management review

TRANSITIONAL PERIODS OF ISO 9001:2015

- The ISO 9001:2015 standard was published on October 25, 2015
- Companies that are certified to ISO 9001:2008 have three years to bring their QMS up to date with ISO 9001:2015
- Eventually all certificates in accordance with ISO 9001:2008 will become invalid and will be withdrawn as of October 25, 2018

CONTEXT OF THE ORGANIZATION AND EXPECTATIONS OF INTERESTED PARTIES

> **ISO 9001:2015 Requirement**
>
> **4.1 Understanding the organization and its context**
>
> The organization shall determine external and internal issues that are relevant to its purpose and its strategic direction and that affect its ability to achieve the intended result(s) of its quality management system. The organization shall monitor and review information about these external and internal issues.
> NOTE 1: Issues can include positive and negative factors or conditions for consideration.
> NOTE 2: Understanding the external context can be facilitated by considering issues arising from legal, technological, competitive, market, cultural, social and economic environments, whether international, national, regional or local.
> NOTE 3: Understanding the internal context can be facilitated by considering issues related to values, culture, knowledge and performance of the organization.

> **ISO 9001:2015 Requirement**
>
> **4.2 Understanding the needs and expectations of interested parties**
>
> Due to their effect or potential effect on the organization's ability to consistently provide products and services that meet customer and applicable statutory and regulatory requirements, the organization shall determine:
>
> a) the interested parties that are relevant to the quality management system;
>
> b) the requirements of these interested parties that are relevant to the quality management system
>
> The organization shall monitor and review information about these interested parties and their relevant requirements.

Considerations for Context and Interested Parties

- What are the internal and external issues that are relevant to the organization's purpose and its strategic direction? *Examples:* Legal, technological, competitive, market, cultural, social, and economic environments, whether international, national, regional, or local

- How does the organization review and monitor the relevant internal and external issues? *Example:* Business planning strategy

- Who/what are the interested parties that are relevant to the QMS? *Examples:* Legal agencies and regulatory bodies, creators of new technology, new competitors

- How does the organization review and monitor the requirements of relevant interested parties? *Example:* Business planning strategy

The following checklists can be used to explore the context of the organization. Review the possible external issues, internal issues, and interested parties on the checklists and check off those that could impact the organization. For each item checked, the organization can develop a plan to manage the risks and opportunities specific to that area.

External issues	Possible impact?	Comments
Product-related regulations	☐	
New technology	☐	
New competition	☐	
Outsourced suppliers	☐	
Supplier vulnerability	☐	
Supplier costs	☐	
Material restrictions	☐	
Energy costs	☐	
Employee healthcare costs	☐	
Employee organizations	☐	
Export tariffs	☐	
Other	☐	

Internal issues	Possible impact?	Comments
Employee turnover	☐	
Retiring employees	☐	
Employee costs	☐	
Aging equipment/facilities	☐	
Employee morale	☐	
Other	☐	

Interested parties	Possible impact?	Comments
Regulatory bodies	☐	
Neighbors	☐	
Community	☐	
Shareholders	☐	
Other	☐	

INTEGRATION OF THE QMS INTO THE BUSINESS PROCESSES

> **ISO 9001:2015 Requirement**
>
> **5.1.1 Leadership and commitment**
>
> Top management shall demonstrate leadership and commitment with respect to the quality management system by:
>
> a) ensuring the integration of the quality management system requirements into the organization's business processes

Summary: Leadership and Commitment

How does the organization's top management integrate the QMS requirements into the organization's business processes?

An organization with an integrated business system is one whose QMS includes control, monitoring, and performance measurements for all relevant business processes.

An example is how the organization measures KPIs. The KPIs for quality performance typically include internal quality or waste, delivery performance, supplier performance, and design performance.

An integrated business system will include KPIs (as appropriate) for financial results and environmental and safety performance.

ACTIONS TO ADDRESS RISKS AND OPPORTUNITIES

> **ISO 9001:2015 Requirement**
>
> 6.1.1: When planning for the quality management system, the organization shall consider the context of the organization and the needs of interested parties.
>
> The organization shall determine the risks and opportunities that need to be addressed to give assurance that the quality management system can:
>
> a) achieve its intended results;
>
> b) enhance desirable effects;
>
> c) prevent, or reduce, undesired effects;
>
> d) achieve improvement

Note: ISO 9001:2015 does not have a requirement for "preventive action." The thought is the entire quality management system is preventive in nature and the risk analysis approach is also preventive.

Summary: Risk Assessment

- How does the organization assess the risks and opportunities related to its purpose, its business strategy, and the expectations of interested parties to ensure the QMS meets its objectives? *Examples:* Strategic planning process, SWOT analysis, Six Sigma, lean manufacturing, FMEA

- What are some examples of how the organization addresses the identified risks and opportunities? *Examples:* Reports or records of risk analysis

Specific areas where risk analysis can be applied include:

- *Process or equipment changes:* When production equipment or processes are changed, the implementation plan should include the potential risk to product quality. Testing a "new" product material prior to release to customers is a common technique employed, along with the application of FMEA.

- *Raw material specification control:* Any change in materials used in production should be tested before release to customers. The organization should ensure its suppliers are aware of the need to communicate and maintain control of any changes in their specifications or processes.

- *Document control and review:* The organization should ensure that documents used by employees are maintained and controlled to avoid mistakes. Employee instructions should be reviewed at some frequency to ensure employees are not bypassing operating instructions.

- *Design:* During the design process, a robust verification and validation plan should be employed to eliminate risks related to new designs. The new design process should also include a risk analysis related to the impact the new design process may have on employee safety and the environment, including end-of-life disposal issues.

- *Regulatory updates:* The organization should maintain a process to stay up to date on changes to statutory and regulatory obligations related to its products to eliminate risks related to noncompliance.

- *Outsourced processes:* Processes performed by external parties can create a risk for the organization in meeting its commitment. External supplier selection should include controls related to the impact the supplier could have on producing acceptable products or services. Inspection of externally supplied products should be based on inspection cost versus risk related to supplier errors.

- *Planning of internal audits:* The timing of internal audits for various processes should be based on the impact the process has on quality performance as well as the history the particular process has of generating nonconformances. By focusing on the history and impact of each process, the organization can allocate auditing resources to reduce the risk of errors.

- *Effectiveness of corrective actions:* An important consideration in the corrective action process is how effectively the correction reduces the risk of the same issue recurring. Time and resources allocated to measuring the effectiveness of the correction should be commensurate with the risk of recurrence.

TOP MANAGEMENT COMMITMENT

> ### ISO 9001:2015 Requirement
>
> **5.3 Organizational roles, responsibilities and authorities**
>
> Top management shall ensure that the responsibilities and authorities for relevant roles are assigned, communicated and understood within the organization.
>
> Top management shall assign the responsibility and authority for: ensuring that the quality management system conforms to the requirements of this International Standard;
>
> a) ensuring that the processes are delivering their intended outputs;
>
> b) reporting on the performance of the quality management system and on opportunities for improvement in particular to top management;
>
> c) ensuring the promotion of customer focus throughout the organization;
>
> d) ensuring that the integrity of the quality management system is maintained when changes to the quality management system are planned and implemented

Top Management Changes with ISO 9001:2015

- The ISO 9001:2015 standard does not use the title "management representative" as previous ISO 9001 standards did

- The organization can continue to use the "management representative" title to convey certain responsibilities

- The intent of ISO 9001:2015 is to emphasize top management's responsibilities as going beyond delegating

Summary: Top Management's Role

- How does top management integrate the QMS requirements into the organization's business processes?

- What is the evidence to indicate that top management provides resources to support the QMS? *Examples:* New equipment, resources

- How does top management promote the use of the process approach and risk-based thinking?

- How does top management communicate the importance of effective quality management and of conformance to the QMS requirements?

- How does top management demonstrate leadership and commitment with respect to customer focus by ensuring that customer requirements and applicable statutory and regulatory requirements are determined, understood, and consistently met?

- How does top management assess the risks and opportunities that can affect conformity of products and services?

Examples of Top Management Commitment

- Do members of top management attend quality management reviews?
- Is the management representative a member of the senior staff?
- Does management provide support for resources necessary to maintain and improve the QMS?

ORGANIZATIONAL KNOWLEDGE

> **ISO 9001:2015 Requirement**
>
> **7.1.6 Organizational knowledge**
>
> The organization shall determine the knowledge necessary for the operation of its processes and to achieve conformity of products and services.
>
> This knowledge shall be maintained and be made available to the extent necessary.
>
> When addressing changing needs and trends, the organization shall consider its current knowledge and determine how to acquire or access any necessary additional knowledge and required updates.
>
> NOTE 1: Organizational knowledge is knowledge specific to the organization; it is generally gained by experience. It is information that is used and shared to achieve the organization's objectives.
>
> NOTE 2: Organizational knowledge can be based on:
>
> a) internal sources (e.g. intellectual property; knowledge gained from experience; lessons learned from failures and successful projects; capturing and sharing undocumented knowledge and experience; the results of improvements in processes, products and services);
>
> b) external sources (e.g. standards; academia; conferences; gathering knowledge from customers or external providers)

Organizational Knowledge Considerations

ISO 9001:2015 requires that organizations *consider* and review the organization's processes to ensure that

- Operational/process or product knowledge is maintained when employees leave the organization
- The organization remains knowledgeable about new technology relevant to its business model

The organization, depending on its operations, should have some formalized program for succession planning, technology updates, and supplier contingencies. Many organizations maintain organizational knowledge through their business strategy and contingency plan.

This information may be confidential, so auditors may not be allowed to see the details—only that the organization has a process for maintaining organizational knowledge.

DOCUMENTATION

Documentation Changes with ISO 9001:2015

- A nomenclature change with ISO 9001:2015 is designating documented information as including both documents and records, which were defined independently in prior ISO 9001 revisions
- There is no requirement in ISO 9001:2015 indicating that organizations cannot use the term "quality record"
- ISO 9000:2015 defines *documented information* as "information required to be controlled and maintained by an organization and the medium on which it is contained"
- According to ISO 9000:2015, "documented information can be in any format and media, and from any source"
- ISO 9000:2015 defines *documents* as "information created in order for the organization to operate"
- ISO 9000:2015 defines *records* as "evidence of results achieved"

ISO 9001:2015 Requirement

7.5.2 Creating and Updating

When creating and updating documented information, the organization shall ensure appropriate:

a) Identification and description (e.g. a title, date, author, or reference number);

b) Format (e.g. language, software version, graphics) and media (e.g. paper, electronic);

c) Review and approval for suitability and adequacy

Note: ISO 9001:2015 is more prescriptive on the formatting of documentation.

PROGRAMS TO ACHIEVE QUALITY OBJECTIVES

Documentation Changes with ISO 9001:2015

- ISO 9001:2015 does not explicitly refer to the requirement for a quality manual
- Organizations that currently maintain a quality manual may want to continue using it as a high-level consolidation of the key elements—or road map—of their quality documentation

Suggested Quality Manual Contents

- A description of the organization's business model, including the context of the organization and the expectations of interested parties

- The scope (the activities, processes, and buildings and locations) of the QMS

- A description of those ISO 9001:2015 requirements that are not applicable to the QMS, as they do not affect the organization's ability or responsibility to ensure the conformity of its products and services

- The documented procedures (documented information) established for the QMS, or reference to them

- A description of the processes in the QMS and how they interact

- The quality policy

- Responsibilities/authorities

ISO 9001:2015 Requirement

6.2.2: When planning how to achieve its quality objectives, the organization shall determine:

a) What will be done; what resources will be required;

b) Who will be responsible;

c) When it will be completed; how the results will be evaluated

---

Summary: Quality Objectives

- Are the quality objectives consistent with the quality policy?

- Are the quality objectives measurable?

- Are the quality objectives relevant to product or service conformity?

- How does the organization communicate the quality objectives to employees?

- In planning to achieve the quality objectives, does the organization establish:

  – What will be done?

  – What resources will be required?

  – Who will be responsible?

  – When it will be completed?

  – How the results will be evaluated?

- How are the quality objectives monitored, and what actions are taken when the objectives are not met?

PREPARING FOR UPGRADE AUDIT TO ISO 9001:2015

- Review and revise scope of QMS:
  - Context of business, internal/external issues
  - Interested parties
- Update quality manual
- Develop risk analysis process
- Develop organizational knowledge process
- Formalize planning to achieve quality objectives
- Management review:
  - Demonstrate integration of QMS with business
  - Review risk analysis and organizational knowledge
  - Review quality objectives programs
- Conduct internal audit to ISO 9001:2015
- Implement corrections from internal audit

Appendix B
Failure Modes and Effects Analysis (FMEA)

Failure modes and effects analysis (FMEA) is a step-by-step approach for identifying all possible failures in a design, a manufacturing or assembly process, or a product or service.

"Failure modes" means the ways, or modes, in which something might fail. Failures are any errors or defects, especially ones that affect the customer, and can be potential or actual.

"Effects analysis" refers to studying the consequences of those failures.

Failures are prioritized according to how serious their consequences are, how frequently they occur and how easily they can be detected. The purpose of the FMEA is to take actions to eliminate or reduce failures, starting with the highest-priority ones.

Failure modes and effects analysis also documents current knowledge and actions about the risks of failures, for use in continuous improvement. FMEA is used during design to prevent failures. Later it's used for control, before and during ongoing operation of the process. Ideally, FMEA begins during the earliest conceptual stages of design and continues throughout the life of the product or service.

Begun in the 1940s by the U.S. military, FMEA was further developed by the aerospace and automotive industries. Several industries maintain formal FMEA standards.

What follows is an overview and reference. Before undertaking an FMEA process, learn more about standards and specific methods in your organization and industry through other references and training.

When to Use FMEA

- When a process, product or service is being designed or redesigned, after quality function deployment.

- When an existing process, product or service is being applied in a new way.

- Before developing control plans for a new or modified process.

- When improvement goals are planned for an existing process, product or service.

- When analyzing failures of an existing process, product or service.

- Periodically throughout the life of the process, product or service.

Excerpted from Nancy R. Tague, *The Quality Toolbox*, 2nd ed. (Milwaukee, WI: ASQ Quality Press, 2004), 236–40.

FMEA Procedure

(Again, this is a general procedure. Specific details may vary with standards of your organization or industry.)

1. Assemble a cross-functional team of people with diverse knowledge about the process, product or service and customer needs. Functions often included are: design, manufacturing, quality, testing, reliability, maintenance, purchasing (and suppliers), sales, marketing (and customers) and customer service.

2. Identify the scope of the FMEA. Is it for concept, system, design, process or service? What are the boundaries? How detailed should we be? Use flowcharts to identify the scope and to make sure every team member understands it in detail. (From here on, we'll use the word "scope" to mean the system, design, process or service that is the subject of your FMEA.)

3. Fill in the identifying information at the top of your FMEA form. Figure B.1 shows a typical format. The remaining steps ask for information that will go into the columns of the form.

4. Identify the functions of your scope. Ask, "What is the purpose of this system, design, process or service? What do our customers expect it to do?" Name it with a verb followed by a noun. Usually you will break the scope into separate subsystems, items, parts, assemblies or process steps and identify the function of each.

5. For each function, identify all the ways failure could happen. These are potential failure modes. If necessary, go back and rewrite the function with more detail to be sure the failure modes show a loss of that function.

6. For each failure mode, identify all the consequences on the system, related systems, process, related processes, product, service, customer or regulations. These are potential effects of failure. Ask, "What does the customer experience because of this failure? What happens when this failure occurs?"

7. Determine how serious each effect is. This is the severity rating, or S. Severity is usually rated on a scale from 1 to 10, where 1 is insignificant and 10 is catastrophic. If a failure mode has more than one effect, write on the FMEA table only the highest severity rating for that failure mode.

8. For each failure mode, determine all the potential root causes. Use tools classified as cause analysis tool, as well as the best knowledge and experience of the team. List all possible causes for each failure mode on the FMEA form.

9. For each cause, determine the occurrence rating, or O. This rating estimates the probability of failure occurring for that reason during the lifetime of your scope. Occurrence is usually rated on a scale from 1 to 10, where 1 is extremely unlikely and 10 is inevitable. On the FMEA table, list the occurrence rating for each cause.

FAILURE MODES AND EFFECTS ANALYSIS (FMEA) 125

Function	Potential failure mode	Potential effect(s) of failure	S	Potential cause(s) of failure	O	Current process controls	D	RPN	CRIT	Recommended action(s)	Responsibility and target completion date	Action taken	Action results S	O	D	RPN	CRIT
Dispense amount of cash requested by customer	Does not dispense cash	Customer very dissatisfied	8	Out of cash	5	Internal low-cash alert	5	200	40								
		Incorrect entry to demand deposit system		Machine jams	3	Internal jam alert	10	240	24								
		Discrepancy in cash balancing		Power failure during transaction	2	None	10	160	16								
	Dispenses too much cash	Bank loses money	6	Bills stuck together	2	Loading procedure (riffle ends of stack)	7	84	12								
		Discrepancy in cash balancing		Denominations in wrong trays	3	Two-person visual verification	4	72	18								
	Takes too long to dispense cash	Customer somewhat annoyed	3	Heavy computer network traffic	7	None	10	210	21								
				Power interruption during transaction	2	None	10	60	6								

Figure B.1 FMEA example.

10. For each cause, identify current process controls. These are tests, procedures or mechanisms that you now have in place to keep failures from reaching the customer. These controls might prevent the cause from happening, reduce the likelihood that it will happen or detect failure after the cause has already happened but before the customer is affected.

11. For each control, determine the detection rating, or D. This rating estimates how well the controls can detect either the cause or its failure mode after they have happened but before the customer is affected. Detection is usually rated on a scale from 1 to 10, where 1 means the control is absolutely certain to detect the problem and 10 means the control is certain not to detect the problem (or no control exists). On the FMEA table, list the detection rating for each cause.

12. (Optional for most industries) Is this failure mode associated with a critical characteristic? (Critical characteristics are measurements or indicators that reflect safety or compliance with government regulations and need special controls.) If so, a column labeled "Classification" receives a Y or N to show whether special controls are needed. Usually, critical characteristics have a severity of 9 or 10 and occurrence and detection ratings above 3.

13. Calculate the risk priority number, or RPN, which equals $S \times O \times D$. Also calculate Criticality by multiplying severity by occurrence, $S \times O$. These numbers provide guidance for ranking potential failures in the order they should be addressed.

14. Identify recommended actions. These actions may be design or process changes to lower severity or occurrence. They may be additional controls to improve detection. Also note who is responsible for the actions and target completion dates.

15. As actions are completed, note results and the date on the FMEA form. Also, note new S, O or D ratings and new RPNs.

FMEA EXAMPLE

A bank performed a process FMEA on their ATM system. Figure B.1 shows part of it—the function "dispense cash" and a few of the failure modes for that function. The optional "Classification" column was not used. Only the headings are shown for the rightmost (action) columns.

Notice that RPN and criticality prioritize causes differently. According to the RPN, "machine jams" and "heavy computer network traffic" are the first and second highest risks.

One high value for severity or occurrence times a detection rating of 10 generates a high RPN. Criticality does not include the detection rating, so it rates highest the only cause with medium to high values for both severity and occurrence: "out of cash." The team should use their experience and judgment to determine appropriate priorities for action.

Appendix C
Stage-Gate® Idea-to-Launch Model

Stage-Gate® is a value-creating business process and risk model designed to quickly and profitably transform an organization's best new ideas into winning new products. When embraced by organizations, it creates a culture of product innovation excellence—product leadership, accountability, high-performance teams, customer and market focus, robust solutions, alignment, discipline, speed and quality.

In addition to the benefits that are well-documented by research and benchmarking firms, many companies that have implemented and adopted an authentic Stage-Gate process realize:

- Accelerated speed-to-market
- Increased new product success rates
- Decreased new product failures
- Increased organizational discipline and focus on the right projects
- Fewer errors, waste and re-work within projects
- Improved alignment across business leaders
- Efficient and effective allocation of scarce resources
- Improved visibility of all projects in the pipeline
- Improved cross-functional engagement and collaboration
- Improved communication and coordination with external stakeholders.

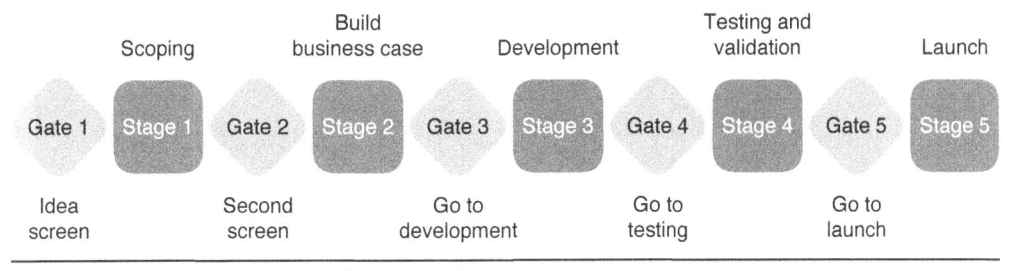

Figure C.1 The Stage-Gate product innovation process.
Source: Adapted with permission from SG Navigator.

Reprinted with permission from Stage-Gate International, "Innovation Process," http://www.stage-gate.com/resources_stage-gate_full.php.

HOW DOES A STAGE-GATE® PROCESS WORK?

The Stage-Gate model is based on the belief that product innovation begins with ideas and ends once a product is successfully launched into the market. This has a lot to do with the benchmarking research that the Stage-Gate model design is premised on, and is a much broader and more cross-functional view of a product development process.

The Stage-Gate model takes the often complex and chaotic process of taking an idea from inception to launch, and breaks it down into smaller stages (where project activities are conducted) and gates (where business evaluations and Go/Kill decisions are made). In its entirety, Stage-Gate incorporates Pre-development Activities (business justification and preliminary feasibilities), Development Activities (technical, marketing, and operations development) and Commercialization Activities (market launch and post launch learning) into one complete, robust process.

THE STAGES

Each stage is designed to collect specific information to help move the project to the next stage or decision point.

Each stage is defined by the activities within it. Activities are completed in parallel (allowing for projects to quickly move towards completion) and are cross-functional (not dominated by any single functional area). These activities are designed to gather information and progressively reduce uncertainty and risk. Each stage is increasingly more costly and emphasizes collection of additional information to reduce uncertainty.

In the typical Stage-Gate model, there are 5 stages, in addition to the Idea Discovery Stage:

Stage 0: Idea Discovery. Pre-work designed to discover and uncover business opportunities and generate new ideas.

Stage 1: Scoping. Quick, inexpensive preliminary investigation and scoping of the project—largely desk research.

Stage 2: Build the Business Case. Detailed investigation involving primary research—both market and technical—leading to a Business Case, including product and project definition, project justification, and the proposed plan for development.

Figure C.2 The stages.
Source: Adapted with permission from SG Navigator.

Stage 3: Development. The actual detailed design and development of the new product and the design of the operations or production process required for eventual full-scale production.

Stage 4: Testing and Validation. Tests or trials in the marketplace, lab, and plant to verify and validate the proposed new product, brand/marketing plan and production/operations.

Stage 5: Launch. Commercialization—beginning of full-scale operations or production, marketing, and selling.

THE GATES

Preceding each stage, a project passes through a gate where a decision is made whether or not to continue investing in the project (a Go/Kill decision). These serve as quality-control checkpoints with three goals: ensure quality of execution, evaluate business rationale, and approve the project plan and resources.

Each gate is structured in a similar way:

Deliverables. The project leader and team provide Gatekeepers with the high-level results of the activities completed during the previous stage.

Criteria. The project is measured against a defined set of success criteria that every new product project is measured against. Criteria should be robust to help screen out winning products, sooner. The authentic Stage-Gate process incorporates 6 proven criteria: Strategic Fit, Product and Competitive Advantage, Market Attractiveness, Technical Feasibility, Synergies/Core Competencies, Financial Reward/Risk.

Outputs. A decision is made (Go/Kill/Hold/Recycle). New product development resources are committed to continuing the project. The action plan for the next stage is approved. A list of deliverables and date for the next gate is set.

The Stage-Gate model is designed to improve the speed and quality of execution of new product development activities. The process helps project teams prepare the right information, with the right level of detail, at the right gate to support the best decision possible, and allocate capital and operating resources. The process empowers the project team by providing them with a roadmap, with clear decisions, priorities, and deliverables at each gate. Higher quality deliverables submitted to Gatekeepers enables timely decisions.

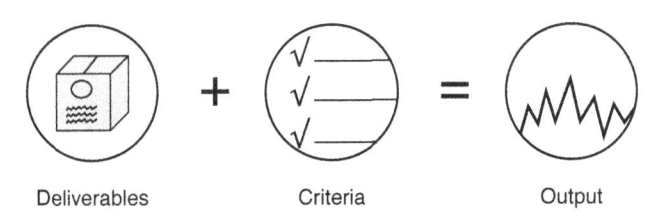

Figure C.3 The gates.
Source: Adapted with permission from SG Navigator.

FLEXIBLE IMPLEMENTATION INTO AN ORGANIZATION

Many top performing organizations report that "making Stage-Gate stick and sustaining it" requires good change management. The authentic Stage-Gate design is sophisticated because it has evolved and benefitted from 25+ years of business and industry benchmarking research and learnings from more company implementations than any other innovation process in the world. For most organizations, the authentic Stage-Gate design represents a goal to work towards: adopting core basic principles initially and continuously embracing more and more of its design as the company's innovation capability improves. In addition to tailoring the Stage-Gate model to accommodate an organization's innovation capability, consider also tailoring it to fit and support the unique needs of your business culture, global strategies, customer types (B2B and B2C), new product strategies, and types of innovation projects.

Appendix D
Quality in Healthcare: Five Whys and Five Hows

What It Is

- The *five whys* and *five hows* constitute a questioning process designed to drill down into the details of a problem or a solution and peel away the layers of symptoms.

- The technique was originally developed by Sakichi Toyoda. He states "that by repeating why five times, the nature of the problem as well as its solution becomes clear."

- The five whys are used for drilling down into a problem and the five *hows* are used to develop the details of a solution to a problem.

- Both are designed to bring clarity and refinement to a problem statement or a potential solution and get to the root cause or root solution.

- Edward Hodnet, a British poet, observed, "If you don't ask the right questions, you don't get the right answers. A question asked in the right way often points to its own answer. Asking questions is the ABC of diagnosis. Only the inquiring mind solves problems."

When to Use It

- When we want to push a team investigating a problem to delve into more details of the root causes, the five whys can be used with brainstorming or the cause-and-effect diagram.

- The five hows can be used with brainstorming and the solution-and-effect diagram to develop more details of a solution to a problem under consideration.

- Both methods are techniques to expand the horizon of a team searching for answers. These two techniques force a team to develop a better and more detailed understanding of a problem or solution.

Excerpted from Ron Bialek, Grace L. Duffy, and John W. Moran, *The Public Health Quality Improvement Handbook* (Milwaukee, WI: ASQ Quality Press, 2009), 168–70.

How to Use It

- Draw a box at the top of a piece of flip chart paper and clearly write down the problem or solution to be explored.

- Below the statement box draw five lines in descending order.

- Ask the "Why" or "How" question five times and write the answers on the lines drawn from number one to five.

- It may take less or more than five times to reach the root cause or solution.

Examples of five whys and five hows are below.

Five whys of less vigorous exercise:

Too much TV and video games	*Why?*
Few community-sponsored recreation programs	*Why?*
No family recreational activities	*Why?*
No safe play area	*Why?*
Lack of resources	*Why?*

Five hows of more vigorous exercise:

Less TV and video games	*How?*
More community-sponsored recreation programs	*How?*
More family recreational activities	*How?*
Safe play areas	*How?*
Additional resources	*How?*

Appendix E
What Is Six Sigma?

Quality Glossary Definition: Six Sigma

A method that provides organizations tools to improve the capability of their business processes. This increase in performance and decrease in process variation lead to defect reduction and improvement in profits, employee morale, and quality of products or services. Six Sigma quality is a term generally used to indicate a process is well controlled (within process limits ±3s from the center line in a control chart, and requirements/tolerance limits ±6s from the center line).

Different definitions have been proposed for Six Sigma, but they all share some common threads:

- Use of teams that are assigned well-defined projects that have direct impact on the organization's bottom line.

- Training in "statistical thinking" at all levels and providing key people with extensive training in advanced statistics and project management. These key people are designated "Black Belts."

- Emphasis on the DMAIC approach to problem solving: Define, measure, analyze, improve, and control.

- A management environment that supports these initiatives as a business strategy.

Differing opinions on the definition of Six Sigma:

Philosophy. The philosophical perspective views all work as processes that can be defined, measured, analyzed, improved and controlled. Processes require inputs (x) and produce outputs (y). If you control the inputs, you will control the outputs. This is generally expressed as y = f(x).

Set of tools. The Six Sigma expert uses qualitative and quantitative techniques to drive process improvement. A few such tools include statistical process control (SPC), control charts, failure mode and effects analysis, and process mapping. Six Sigma professionals do not totally agree as to exactly which tools constitute the set.

Excerpted from T. M. Kubiak and Donald W. Benbow, *The Certified Six Sigma Black Belt Handbook*, 2nd ed. (Milwaukee, WI: ASQ Quality Press, 2009), 6–7.

Methodology. This view of Six Sigma recognizes the underlying and rigorous approach known as DMAIC (define, measure, analyze, improve and control). DMAIC defines the steps a Six Sigma practitioner is expected to follow, starting with identifying the problem and ending with the implementation of long-lasting solutions. While DMAIC is not the only Six Sigma methodology in use, it is certainly the most widely adopted and recognized.

Metrics. In simple terms, Six Sigma quality performance means 3.4 defects per million opportunities (accounting for a 1.5-sigma shift in the mean).

Appendix F
What Is Lean?

Henry Ford defined the lean concept in one sentence: "We will not put into our establishment anything that is useless."

Lean manufacturing is a system of techniques and activities for running a manufacturing or service operation. The techniques and activities differ according to the application at hand but they have the same underlying principle: the elimination of all non-value-adding activities and waste from the business.

Lean enterprise extends this concept through the entire value stream or supply chain: The leanest factory cannot achieve its full potential if it has to work with non-lean suppliers and subcontractors.

Types of Waste

1. Overproduction
2. Waiting, time in queue
3. Transportation
4. Non-value-adding processes
5. Inventory
6. Motion
7. Costs of quality: scrap, rework and inspection

Excerpted from William A. Levinson and Raymond A. Rerick, *Lean Enterprise: A Synergistic Approach to Minimizing Waste* (Milwaukee, WI: ASQ Quality Press, 2002), xiii–xiv, 38.

Appendix G
Context of the Organization: Checklists for External and Internal Issues and Interested Parties

Consider which of the following external issues could impact the organization:

External issues	Possible impact?	Comments
Product-related regulations	☐	
New technology	☐	
New competition	☐	
Outsourced suppliers	☐	
Supplier vulnerability	☐	
Supplier costs	☐	
Material restrictions	☐	
Energy costs	☐	
Employee healthcare costs	☐	
Employee organizations	☐	
Export tariffs	☐	
Other	☐	

Consider which of the following internal issues could impact the organization:

Internal issues	Possible impact?	Comments
Employee turnover	☐	
Retiring employees	☐	
Employee costs	☐	
Aging equipment/facilities	☐	
Employee morale	☐	
Other	☐	

Consider what outside groups could impact the organization:

Interested parties	Possible impact?	Comments
Regulatory bodies	☐	
Neighbors	☐	
Community	☐	
Shareholders	☐	
Other	☐	

References

Automotive Industry Action Group (AIAG). 2006. *Production Part Approval Process (PPAP).* 4th ed.

Balestracci, Davis. 2009. "Why Did Total Quality Management Fail?" *Quality Digest*, August 6. http://www.qualitydigest.com/read/content_by_author/11300?page=9.

Borror, Connie M., ed. 2009. *The Certified Quality Engineer Handbook.* 3rd ed. Milwaukee, WI: ASQ Quality Press.

Champy, James, and Michael Hammer. 1993. *Reengineering the Corporation: A Manifesto for Business Revolution.* New York: HarperBusiness.

Kubiak, T. M., and Donald W. Benbow. 2009. *The Certified Six Sigma Black Belt Handbook.* 2nd ed. Milwaukee, WI: ASQ Quality Press.

Valdes-Dapena, Peter. 2014. "GM Recall Was Delayed by Internal Miscues." CNNMoney, February 28. http://money.cnn.com/2014/02/28/autos/gm-recall-timeline.

Vista Industrial Products. 2012. "Fit, Form, Function Explained." March 23. http://www.vista-industrial.com/blog/fit-form-function-explained.

Index

Note: Page numbers followed by *f* or *t* refer to figures or tables, respectively.

A

act (PDCA), 85. *See also* improvement, of ISO 9001:2015
American National Standards Institute (ANSI), 61
American Society for Quality (ASQ)
    guidance on FMEA process, 34
    lean manufacturing programs, 103
    risk-based thinking resources, 36
    Six Sigma, 103
    website, 34
American Society for Testing Materials (ASTM), 61
Annex A to ISO 9001:2015
    documented information, 109–111
    structure and terminology, 108–111, 109*t*
appendices
    Context of the Organization Checklists (Appendix G), 137–138
    Failure Modes and Effects Analysis (Appendix B), 123–126
    Gap Analysis (Appendix A), 113–122
    Lean (Appendix F), 135
    Quality in Healthcare (Appendix D), 131–132
    Six Sigma (Appendix E), 133–134
    Stage-Gate® Idea-to-Launch Model (Appendix C), 127–130
ASQ/ANSI/ISO 9001:2015, 13–14
audits
    check sheets, 93, 94*f*
    confidentiality in, 9, 17, 45, 50, 120
    of context of organization, 16–17, 17–18, 23
    examples of, 34–35, 36–37, 41, 52, 53–54, 64, 78, 96
    of improvement, 102, 104
    of leadership, 26–27, 29, 31
    nonconformance criteria, 10–11
    of operations, 62–63, 67–68, 71, 76–77, 83–84
    of performance evaluation, 89, 95, 97
    of planning, 39, 40, 41–42
    of support processes, 47, 49, 52–53, 54–55
    turtle diagram approach, 92–93, 92*f*
    unacceptability of verbal discussion, 108, 110
authority, defined, 30
automobile sector
    Production Part Approval Process (PPAP), 52
awareness, 48, 48*t*

B

business management system (BMS), 26, 96. *See also* leadership, of ISO 9001:2015
business process reengineering (BPR), 36, 37

C

certificate of analysis (COA), 35, 71
certificate of conformance (COC), 71
Champy, James, 37
check (PDCA), 85. *See also* performance evaluation, of ISO 9001:2015
check sheets, in audits, 93, 94*f*
communication, 48, 48*t*
competence, 48, 48*t*, 92
confidentiality
    in audits, 9, 17, 45
    in documented information, 50, 120
continual improvement, 102–104
Cooper, Robert G., 65
corrective action, 100–102, 100*t*
cultural change, 36–38
customers
    communications with, 59

142 Index

leadership role and, 26
property belonging to, 72, 107
satisfaction feedback, 87, 88–89

D

distributors, 80
DMAIC process, 103, 133–134
document, defined, 51
documented information
    Annex A to ISO 9001:2015, 109–111
    defined, 50
    improvement, 100
    support, 49–55

E

effectiveness, defined, 97, 101–102
engineering change notice (ECN), 21–22, 41
external document control, 50, 51
externally provided processes, products, services, 58, 68–71, 69*f*

F

failure modes and effects analysis (FMEA), 8, 34, 38, 108, 123–126
find-and-fix corrective actions, 100, 100*t*
fit, of parts, 52
Five Hows, 131–132
Five Whys, 101, 131–132
form, of parts, 52
function, of parts, 52

G

Gantt charts, 64
General Motors (GM), 51–52

H

Hammer, Michael, 37

I

improvement, of ISO 9001:2015, 99–104
    act (PDCA), 85
    continual improvement, 102–104
    DMAIC process, 103, 133–134
    Five Whys, 101
    general improvement, 99

nonconformity and corrective action, 100–102, 100*t*
    root cause analysis, 101
    Six Sigma, 102–103
information, defined, 110
internal auditors, 92–93
internal audits, 90–95, 91*t*, 92–94*f*, 106
International Organization for Standardization (ISO), 1. *See also headings at* ISO 9001
interpretation guidance, of ISO 9001:2015, 105–111
    Clause 6.1, actions to address risks and opportunities, 105–108
    terminology changes, 108–111
ISO 9000, 1–3, 108
ISO 9001, 1–3, 99
ISO 9001:2000, 2, 3, 19*f*
ISO 9001:2008, 2, 11, 14, 17, 20, 74–75, 86, 86–87
ISO 9001:2015
    clause applicability for service providers, 79*t*
    requirements of, 13–14
    scope of, 1, 3
ISO 9001:2015, Clause 4, 15–24, 79*t*
    4.1, understanding the organization and its context, 15
    4.2, understanding needs and expectations of interested parties, 15–16
    4.2.3, obsolete documents, 35
    4.3, determining scope of QMS, 17–18
    4.4, quality management system and processes, 18–23, 19–22*f*, 86
    4.4.1, process management and flowcharts, 22–23, 22*f*, 86–87
ISO 9001:2015, Clause 5, 25–31, 79*t*
    5.1, leadership and commitment, 8, 25–27, 96
    5.1.1, general role of leadership, 25–26
    5.1.2, customer focus, 26
    5.2, quality policy, 27–29
    5.2.1, establishment of quality policy, 27
    5.2.2, communication of quality policy, 27
    5.3, organizational roles, responsibilities and authorities, 30–31
ISO 9001:2015, Clause 6, 33–42, 79*t*
    6.1, actions to address risks and opportunities, 33–39, 105–108
    6.1.1, assurance of achievement of QMS objectives, 33, 105–106

Index 143

6.1.2, organizational planning, 33, 105–106
6.2, quality objectives and processes, 39–40
6.2.1, establishment of quality objectives, 39
6.2.2, planning actions to achieve objectives, 10, 39
6.3, change control processes, 40–42
ISO 9001:2015, Clause 7, 43–55, 44f, 79t
   7.1, support resources, 44–47
   7.1.1, general, 44
   7.1.2, people, 44
   7.1.3, infrastructure, 44, 80
   7.1.4, operational environment, 44
   7.1.5, monitoring and measurement of resources, 44–45
   7.1.5.1, reliability and validity in measurement, 44
   7.1.5.2, measurement of traceability, 45
   7.1.6, organizational knowledge, 45
   7.2, competence, 48, 48t, 92
   7.3, awareness, 48, 48t
   7.4, communication, 48, 48t
   7.5, documented information, 49–55
   7.5.1, general, 49
   7.5.2, creating/updating documented information, 49, 50
   7.5.3, control of documented information, 50, 51
   7.5.3.1, objectives of control of documented information, 50
   7.5.3.2, activities in control of documented information, 50
ISO 9001:2015, Clause 8, 57–84, 58f, 79t
   8.1, operational planning and control, 59, 106
   8.2, product and service requirements, 59–63
   8.2.1, customer communications, 59
   8.2.2, determination of product/service requirements, 59–60
   8.2.3, review of product/service requirements, 60–61
   8.2.4, changes to product/service requirements, 61
   8.3, product and service design and development, 63–68, 65–66f, 67t
   8.3.1, general, 63
   8.3.2, design and development planning, 63
   8.3.3, design and development inputs, 63–64
   8.3.4, design and development controls, 64
   8.3.5, design and development outputs, 64
   8.3.6, design and development changes, 64
   8.4, control of externally provided processes, products, services, 58, 68–71, 69f
   8.4.1, general, 68
   8.4.2, type and extent of control, 68–69
   8.4.3, information for external providers, 69
   8.5, production and service provision, 72–73, 74f, 106, 107
   8.5.1, control of production/service provision, 72, 82
   8.5.2, identification and traceability, 72, 107
   8.5.3, customer/external provider property, 72, 107
   8.5.4, preservation, 72, 75, 106
   8.5.5, post-delivery activities, 73
   8.5.6, control of changes, 73
   8.6, release of products/services, 73
   8.7, control of nonconforming outputs, 73–77, 74f
   8.7.1, identification of nonconforming outputs, 73
   service provisions and, 78–84, 79t, 81f, 82t
ISO 9001:2015, Clause 9, 79t, 85–97, 86f
   9.1, monitoring, measurement, analysis and evaluation, 86–89, 86f
   9.1.1, general, 87
   9.1.2, customer satisfaction, 87, 88–89
   9.1.3, analysis and evaluation, 87, 89
   9.2, internal audits, 90–95, 91t, 92–94f, 106
   9.2.1, general internal audit, 90
   9.2.2, internal audit programs, 90, 91
   9.3, management review, 95–97
   9.3.1, general, 95
   9.3.2, management review inputs, 95–96
   9.3.3, management review outputs, 96
ISO 9001:2015, Clause 10, 79t, 86f, 99–104
   10.1, improvement, 99
   10.2, nonconformity and corrective action, 100–102, 100t
   10.2.1, corrective action, 100
   10.2.2, documented information, 100
   10.3, continual improvement, 102–104
ISO 9001:2015, requirements, 13–14
   Clauses 4–10, 14
   normative references, 14
   scope of, 13–14
   terms and definitions, 14, 108–111
ISO 9001:2015, summary of changes, 6–11, 109t. *See also* interpretation guidance, of ISO 9001:2015
   auditing notes, 10–11
   change to monitoring and measurement of processes, 85–86

change to validation of processes, 74–75
clause numbering and document formats, 9–10
context and interested parties, 7
Gap Analysis (Appendix A), 113–122
integration of QMS into business processes, 7
metrics, 86–87
organizational knowledge, 8–9
preventive actions, 99
quality objectives implementation, 10
risk analysis, 7–8
top management commitment, 8
transitional periods, 11
ISO 9002, 1
ISO 9003, 1
ISO 14001, 5
ISO 14001:2015, 9, 10, 13, 50, 109

J

Juran, Joseph, 103

K

Kanter, Rosabeth Moss, 37
key performance indicators (KPIs), 7

L

lawsuits, 51, 109
leadership, of ISO 9001:2015, 25–31
    commitment of, 8, 25–27, 96
    customer focus, 26
    organizational roles, responsibilities and authorities, 30–31
    prevention of management overdelegation, 8, 30
    quality policy, 27–29
    risk-based thinking, 25–26
lean manufacturing programs, 8, 34, 37–38, 99, 103, 108
likelihood of occurrence, 36

M

management representative, use of term, 30
management review, 95–97
metrics, 61–62, 62t, 76, 82, 86–87
middle managers, 37–38
mission, defined, 27

N

National Electrical Manufacturers Association (NEMA), 61
nonconformity and corrective action, 10–11, 73–77, 74f, 93–94, 100–102, 100t

O

obsolete documents, 35
on-time delivery (OTD) metrics, 76, 82
operation, of ISO 9001:2015, 57–84
    control of externally provided processes, products, services, 58, 68–71, 69f
    control of nonconforming outputs, 73–77, 74f
    control of production/service provision, 82
    customer communication, 59, 60
    metrics, 61–62, 62t, 76, 82
    operational planning and control, 59, 106
    post-delivery activities, 73, 76
    preservation, 72, 75
    process validation, 74–75
    product and service design and development, 63–68, 65–66f, 80
    product and service requirements, 59–63, 60f
    production and service provision, 72–73, 74f, 106, 107
    purchase order authorization, 71
    purchased price variance (PPV), 71
    release of products/services, 73, 74f
    service provisions, 78–84, 79t, 81f, 82t
    Stage-Gate® Idea-to-Launch Model, 65, 66f, 67, 67t, 80, 127–130
    supplier review process, 70–71
    time-bound plans, 64
opportunities for improvement (OFIs), 93–94
organizational context, of ISO 9001:2015, 18–23, 19–21f
    checklists, 137–138
    determining scope of QMS, 17–18
    documented information, 18–19
    engineering change notice (ECN), 22
    process flow and interactions charts, 19–22, 19–22f
    quality management system and processes, 18–23, 19–22f, 86
    risk analysis, 18
    support processes, 22–23

understanding needs and expectations of interested parties, 15–16
understanding the organization and its context, 15
original equipment manufacturer (OEM), 70–71
outsourcing, defined, 70
overdelegation, 8, 30

P

PDCA (plan-do-check-act) cycle, 5, 5f, 85
performance evaluation, of ISO 9001:2015, 85–97
    check (PDCA), 85
    customer satisfaction, 87, 88–89
    internal audits, 90–95, 91t, 92–94f, 106
    management review, 95–97
    monitoring, measurement, analysis and evaluation, 86–89, 86f
phase-gate. See Stage-Gate® Idea-to-Launch Model
plan-do-check-act (PDCA) approach, 5, 5f, 85
planning, of ISO 9001:2015, 33–42
    actions to address risks and opportunities, 33–39, 105–108
    assurance of achievement of QMS objectives, 105
    change control processes, 40–42
    cultural change, 36–38
    customer focus, 26
    organizational planning, 33, 105–106
    preventive actions, 34
    process or equipment changes, 38
    quality objectives and processes, 10, 39–40
    quality policy, 27
    raw material specification control, 35, 38
    risk-based thinking, 25, 26, 36–39, 107–108
Polaroid Corporation, 36–37, 41
preservation, 72, 75, 106
process flow and interactions charts, 19–22, 19–22f
process-based audits, 90–95, 91t, 92–93f
product, defined, 14
product and service design and development, 63–68, 65–66f, 67t
production and service provision, 72–73, 74f, 106, 107
Production Part Approval Process (PPAP), in automobile sector, 52
purchase order authorization, 71
purchased price variance (PPV), 71

Q

quality circles, 36–37
quality inspections, 75
quality management system, of ISO 9001:2015
    plan-do-check-act (PDCA) approach, 5, 5f
    as process, 5–11, 6f
    requirements of, 13–14
    summary of changes, 6–11
quality manuals, 110
quality policy, 27–29
quality records/list, 51–53, 54t, 109

R

raw material specification control, 35, 38
record, defined, 51
records list. See quality records/list
Reengineering the Corporation (Champy and Hammer), 37
"reference only" notations, 53–54
responsibility, defined, 30
risk registers/logs, 36
risk-based thinking, 25–26, 36–39, 107–108
root cause analysis, 101

S

service, defined, 14
service provider types, 78, 79–82, 79t
service provision equity, 58. *See also* operation, of ISO 9001:2015
severity calculations, 36
Six Sigma, 8, 34, 37–38, 99, 102–103, 108, 133–134
software development, 80–81, 81f, 82t
Stage-Gate® Idea-to-Launch Model, 65, 66f, 67, 67t, 80, 127–130
Stage-Gate International, 65
strategic planning processes, 8, 33–34
strengths-weaknesses-opportunities-threats (SWOT) analysis, 8, 34, 108
suitability and adequacy, 49, 50, 96–97
suppliers
    agreements with, 41
    review process for, 70–71
support, of ISO 9001:2015, 43–55
    approval process, 50
    awareness, 48, 48t
    communication, 48, 48t
    competence, 48, 48t, 92

creating/updating documented information, 49, 50
documented information, 49–55
external document control, 50, 51
misapplication of document control, 53–54
multiple sign-off on documents, 50
suitability and adequacy, 49, 50, 96–97
support resources, 44–47, 80
third-party consultants, 50
work instructions priority list, 51
support resources, 44–47

T

third-party certification, 78
third-party consultants
    misapplication of document control, 53–54
    support resource approvals and, 50
TickIT scheme certification program, 82
time-bound plans, 64
tip sheets, 53

total quality management (TQM), 36, 37
traceability, 45, 72, 107
training
    for internal auditors, 92–93
    in root cause analysis, 101
transitional periods, 11
traveler, 75
turtle diagram audit approach, 92–93, 92*f*

U

U.S. Food and Drug Administration (FDA), 61

V

vision, defined, 27
Vista Industrial Products, 52

W

work instructions priority list, 51

About the Author

Milton Dentch was born and raised in the Worcester, Massachusetts, area. He has a BS in mechanical engineering from Worcester Polytechnic Institute and an MS in quality management systems from the National Graduate School of Quality Management (NGS). After college, he worked as an engineer in the paper industry for five years, and then he worked as an engineer and manager at the Polaroid Corporation in Waltham, Massachusetts, for 27 years. He was also plant manager for the Custom Coating and Laminating plant in Worcester for the Furon Corporation. Milt has over 40 years' experience in a wide variety of industries, including pulp and paper, chemical, plastic and rubber processing, battery manufacturing, converting, electronics assembly, and machine building.

Milt currently provides consulting, training, and auditing related to the International Organization for Standardization requirements for quality, environmental, and safety management systems. He has conducted over 500 audits worldwide for large and small companies. His clients have been as diverse as a floating oil rig in the Gulf of Mexico to an electronics manufacturer in the Ukraine with 4000 employees. Milt is an RABQSA qualified Lead Auditor for Quality and Environmental Management Systems and a Registrar approved OHSAS 18001 Lead Auditor.

In 2012, Milt wrote *Fall of an Icon—Polaroid after Edwin H. Land* (Riverhaven Books), an insider's history of the Polaroid Corporation. His book *The ISO 14001:2015 Implementation Handbook* was published by ASQ Quality Press in 2016.

The Knowledge Center
www.asq.org/knowledge-center

Learn about quality. Apply it. Share it.

ASQ's online Knowledge Center is the place to:

- Stay on top of the latest in quality with Editor's Picks and Hot Topics.
- Search ASQ's collection of articles, books, tools, training, and more.
- Connect with ASQ staff for personalized help hunting down the knowledge you need, the networking opportunities that will keep your career and organization moving forward, and the publishing opportunities that are the best fit for you.

Use the Knowledge Center Search to quickly sort through hundreds of books, articles, and other software-related publications.

www.asq.org/knowledge-center

TRAINING   CERTIFICATION   CONFERENCES   MEMBERSHIP   **PUBLICATIONS**

ASQ
The Global Voice of Quality®

Ask a Librarian

Did you know?

- The ASQ Quality Information Center contains a wealth of knowledge and information available to ASQ members and non-members

- A librarian is available to answer research requests using ASQ's ever-expanding library of relevant, credible quality resources, including journals, conference proceedings, case studies and Quality Press publications

- ASQ members receive free internal information searches and reduced rates for article purchases

- You can also contact the Quality Information Center to request permission to reuse or reprint ASQ copyrighted material, including journal articles and book excerpts

- For more information or to submit a question, visit
http://asq.org/knowledge-center/ ask-a-librarian-index

Visit www.asq.org/qic for more information.

TRAINING   CERTIFICATION   CONFERENCES   MEMBERSHIP   **PUBLICATIONS**

ASQ
The Global Voice of Quality®

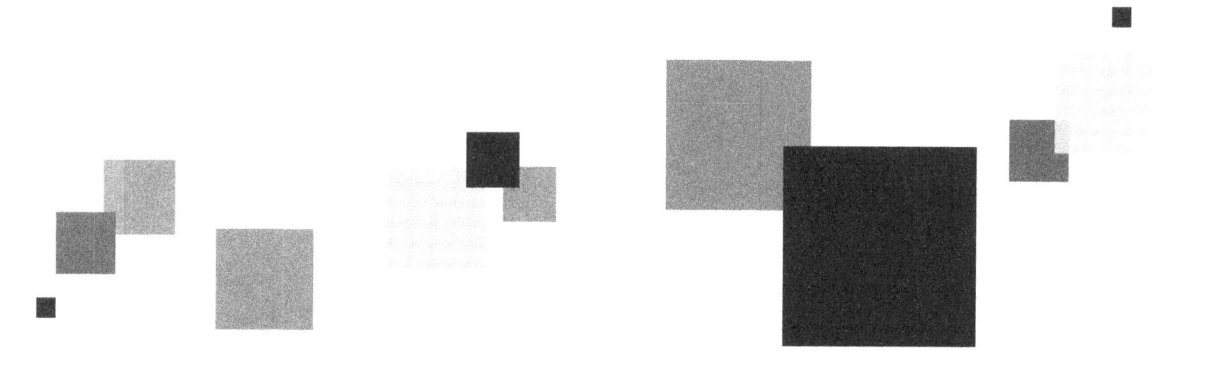

Belong to the Quality Community!

Established in 1946, ASQ is a global community of quality experts in all fields and industries. ASQ is dedicated to the promotion and advancement of quality tools, principles, and practices in the workplace and in the community.

The Society also serves as an advocate for quality. Its members have informed and advised the U.S. Congress, government agencies, state legislatures, and other groups and individuals worldwide on quality-related topics.

Vision

By making quality a global priority, an organizational imperative, and a personal ethic, ASQ becomes the community of choice for everyone who seeks quality technology, concepts, or tools to improve themselves and their world.

ASQ is...

- More than 90,000 individuals and 700 companies in more than 100 countries
- The world's largest organization dedicated to promoting quality
- A community of professionals striving to bring quality to their work and their lives
- The administrator of the Malcolm Baldrige National Quality Award
- A supporter of quality in all sectors including manufacturing, service, healthcare, government, and education
- YOU

Visit www.asq.org for more information.

TRAINING   CERTIFICATION   CONFERENCES   MEMBERSHIP   **PUBLICATIONS**

ASQ
The Global Voice of Quality®

ASQ Membership

Research shows that people who join associations experience increased job satisfaction, earn more, and are generally happier*. ASQ membership can help you achieve this while providing the tools you need to be successful in your industry and to distinguish yourself from your competition. So why wouldn't you want to be a part of ASQ?

Networking

Have the opportunity to meet, communicate, and collaborate with your peers within the quality community through conferences and local ASQ section meetings, ASQ forums or divisions, ASQ Communities of Quality discussion boards, and more.

Professional Development

Access a wide variety of professional development tools such as books, training, and certifications at a discounted price. Also, ASQ certifications and the ASQ Career Center help enhance your quality knowledge and take your career to the next level.

Solutions

Find answers to all your quality problems, big and small, with ASQ's Knowledge Center, mentoring program, various e-newsletters, *Quality Progress* magazine, and industry-specific products.

Access to Information

Learn classic and current quality principles and theories in ASQ's Quality Information Center (QIC), *ASQ Weekly* e-newsletter, and product offerings.

Advocacy Programs

ASQ helps create a better community, government, and world through initiatives that include social responsibility, Washington advocacy, and Community Good Works.

Visit www.asq.org/membership for more information on ASQ membership.

*2008, The William E. Smith Institute for Association Research

TRAINING   CERTIFICATION   CONFERENCES   **MEMBERSHIP**   **PUBLICATIONS**

ASQ
The Global Voice of Quality®